HELPING KIDS CARE

DEAR ABBY: You recently reminded your readers about International Forgiveness Week, which is a wonderful idea. However, it is nothing new. In the Jewish religion, there has been a "forgiveness fortnight" for at least 2,000 years.

During the 10 days between Rosh Hashanah and Yom Kippur, those of the Jewish faith are commanded to ask forgiveness from those whom they may have offended or wronged during the year. In Judaism, God cannot forgive the sins a person has committed against another unless the sinner has asked that person for forgiveness. If the injured party rejects the apology three times, the wrongdoer is then released from his or her obligation to ask forgiveness.

Isn't this a beautiful tradition, as well as a good way to begin a new year?.
— ESTHER KRISMAN, LOS ANGELES

DEAR ESTHER: It is indeed. This year, the 10 days to ask forgiveness are between Sept. 20 and Sept. 29.

DEAR ABBY: Just a note regarding Forgiveness Week. A long time ago I heard the following on, of all shows, "Saturday Night Live":
"Don't hold a grudge,
"It's heavy,
"And it doesn't have a handle."
Worked for me! It can work for everybody.
— SUSIE JOHNSTON-FORTE, ROSEBURG, ORE.

Camy Condon is a writer, adult literacy teacher, and a community puppeteer. Nine of her books on crafts and culture have been published in Japan. During ten years in Tokyo, she wrote a regular newspaper column, performed multicultural puppetry, and founded the Association of English Teachers of Children. She has been a lecturer and performer in Tanzania, Brazil, and Canada, and was invited by the Japanese government to design and participate in dramatic programs for the International Year of Disabled Persons. She is currently the Multicultural Consultant for Puppeteers of America. Much of her present work is concerned with peace and social justice education. She lives with her husband and two teenage children in Albuquerque, N.M., where she is developing Intergenerational Programs for senior citizens and youth.

James McGinnis is founder and director of the Institute for Peace and Justice in St. Louis, Missouri, and is co-coordinator with his wife, Kathleen, of the Parenting for Peace and Justice Network. He is the author of many books and audio-visual resources for parents, teachers, and families, including *Parenting for Peace and Justice,* a three-volume teachers manual entitled *Educating for Peace and Justice,* and the *Building Shalom Families* video program. Thanks to some initial direction and inspiration from Camy Condon, he began using puppets in his peace education work with children and families in 1983 and is now doing this also as "Francis the Clown."

Nanette Ford, a free-lance artist, has been illustrating newspapers, brochures, and books for the past thirteen years. She lives in Webster Groves, Missouri, with her spouse, Jim (who did the layout for this book), and their three children, Aaron, Amy, and Melissa.

HELPING KIDS CARE

Harmony-Building Activities
for Home, Church and School

CAMY CONDON
and
JAMES McGINNIS

Illustrated by Nanette Ford

A Joint Publication of

 The Institute for Peace and Justice

and

BOOKS

Published in the United States by Meyer-Stone Books,
a division of Meyer, Stone, and Company, Inc.,
2014 Yost, Bloomington, IN 47403
and
the Institute for Peace and Justice
4144 Lindell, #122, St. Louis, MO 63108

Cover design: Carol Evans-Smith
Cover photo: Irene O'Neill
Back cover photo: The Institute for
                  Peace and Justice

Manufactured in the United States of America
92 91 90 89 88   5 4 3 2 1

Library of Congress Cataloging in Publication Data

Condon, Camy.
    Helping kids care.

    Includes bibliographies.
    1. Intercultural education — United States.
2. Peace — Study and teaching — United States.
3. Intergenerational relations — Study and teaching —
United States.   4. Discrimination — Study and teaching —
United States.   5. Activity programs in education —
United States.   I. McGinnis, James B.   II. Institute
for Peace and Justice (U.S.)   III. Title.
LC1099.3.C65   1988   370.19'6   88-42725
ISBN 0-940989-24-7

Contents

HOW TO USE THIS BOOK

Progression of Themes

This book begins with "Peacemaking" because most children need to experience peace and justice right where they are. They all experience interpersonal conflict and need to see nonviolent alternatives at that level before getting into larger social issues. Thus, the initial chants and skits focus primarily on nonviolent conflict resolution on the interpersonal level. Later activities include an application to the international level as well. The final four or five focus directly on war, the arms race, and what children can do for world peace. Not all these skits and chants are appropriate to all grade levels and not all those that are appropriate to a particular level need be done. However, it would be good to include at least one from each of the three categories identified above. It is important to include at least one skit or chant that leads the children to some action for peace, at either the interpersonal or international level, but preferably at both levels.

Part II on "Global Awareness" builds on the international dimensions of Part I. The opening WORLD IN A BASKET activity provides the opportunity for various "trips around the world," highlighting peoples and countries and creating a context and an environment for the more specific chants and skits that follow. Two chants, EAT WITH A SPOON and BREAD/RICE FOR THE WORLD, focus attention on specific cultures and customs and open up the issue of differences among the members of our global family, as well as our commonalities. 100 HUNGRY PEOPLE and WHERE'S IT FROM? move the focus from appreciating differences to some of the economic injustices in our global family and challenge participants to identify what they can do to address these injustices. RABBIT IN THE MOON raises the issue of how far we are willing to go in addressing these injustices.

The "multicultural education" dimension to Part II challenges children's stereotypes of people from different cultures. Parts III and IV continue this focus on countering prevalent stereotypes and the injustices that generally flow from stereotyping. Part III, on "Aging Awareness," addresses the issue of "age-ism" — the "writing off," as it were, of older people in our society. People of all ages have much to learn from one another. Part IV, on "Disability Awareness," challenges our concepts of "perfection" and "normal" and promotes a greater sensitivity to the situations of persons with various disabilities. Thus we come full circle to the opening theme of "peacemaking": people of different skills — as well as people of different cultures and different ages — learning how to appreciate one another and work together more cooperatively.

Components of the Activities

1. *Theme and Format* identifies the subject matter, the kind of participatory activity, and its relationship to other activities in the book.

2. *Directions* gives you as leader a step-by-step description of how to lead the activity. (Most of the skits on peacemaking and global awareness are demonstrated on two videotapes, *Puppets for Peace* and *Global Family Puppets,* see below, pp. 2–3.) But do not feel bound by the directions; be as creative in adapting each activity to your own situation as possible.

3. *Discussion Questions* offers you ways of drawing out the learning potential of each activity. Again, adapt the language and questions to the specifics of your situation, using those that are most helpful and not feeling obliged to go through every question listed.

4. *Follow-up Activities* is designed to provide further learning from each activity. Several of the skits and chants are also designed to generate action on the theme. Be selective about which skits or chants to concentrate on and about which follow-up activities to include. Time is a real factor. Be creative and adapt or develop your own.

5. *Further Resources* lists children's books on the theme, as well as one or more key teacher's manuals.

1

Since most of the themes are integral parts of the Institute for Peace and Justice's own three-volume teacher's manual, *Educating for Peace and Justice,* references are also given to the appropriate units in these volumes.

Appropriateness for
Specific Disciplines and Settings

Social Studies

JAPANESE FARM WOMAN in Part I and THE WORLD IN A BASKET, WHERE'S IT FROM?, and the three chants in Part II offer numerous opportunities for geography lessons. Historical follow-up activities are presented with THE RABBIT IN THE MOON. Some basic economics can be done with 100 HUNGRY PEOPLE. The themes of hunger, poverty, and global interdependence are current events/social issues that children are able to grasp, at least to some extent. And every activity in this part deals with other peoples and cultures.

In Part I, history teachers have four skits that include historical data. JAPANESE FARM WOMAN focuses on the August 6, 1945, bombing of Hiroshima. TWO FLAGS images the developments of the "Cold War" and arms race and projects a future scenario, as does STICKS AND STONES AND THE DRAGON. FRIENDS AND ENEMIES illustrates historical changes between World War II and the present. There are a variety of current events or social issues addressed: interpersonal conflict resolution, cooperation and competition, war and the arms race, international cooperation or interdependence, U.S.-U.S.S.R. relations, peacemaking at all levels, handicap awareness, aging and ageism.

Language Arts

Children can be encouraged to write their own chants, verses, poems, stories, and essays in response to many of the skits and chants.

Foreign Languages

Several languages — Portuguese, Swahili, and Japanese — are illustrated in the activities (or on the videotapes) and can serve as a stepping-off point for further language work. A number of the children's books in the multicultural bibliography in Part II are in languages other than English.

Visual and Performing Arts

Children can be encouraged to draw their responses to the skits and chants; to write and perform their own chants and skits; to design and make puppets, sets, banners, and costumes; or to create a dance or musical interpretation of a skit or chant.

Religious Education

The theme of each skit or chant has an implicit religious dimension that can easily be made explicit. Some specific biblical reflection and religiously oriented teacher resources are provided in THE RABBIT IN THE MOON, JAPANESE FARM WOMAN, and THE THREE LITTLE PIGS AND THE WOLF.

Intergenerational Workshops and Camps

Peace and justice programs or religious education programs for whole families will find these skits and chants an exciting and engaging addition. They are being used by workshop leaders and religious educators doing "Parenting for Peace and Justice" family camps, family retreats, and single-session as well as multi-session programs. For a whole series of workshop models for such intergenerational settings into which these skits and chants could be incorporated, see *Families Peacing It Together: Family Workshop Models for Leaders* (Institute for Peace and Justice and Meyer-Stone Books, forthcoming).

"Puppets for Peace" and
"Global Family Puppets" Videotapes

Children's Performances

This book is best used in conjunction with *Puppets for Peace* and *Global Family Puppets,* two videotapes on which puppeteer Camy Condon demonstrates, unrehearsed and with a live audience, most of the skits and chants described in this book. You see her simple techniques and resources and how she works with children of various ages (mostly 5 through 12), including helping them through their "mistakes." As many have stated, "After seeing Camy do it, I really think I can too!"

Teacher Instruction

In addition to the 35 minutes of skits and chants, each videotape presents a 15-minute discussion between Camy and a group of teachers and workshop leaders present for the children's skits. In this segment, she explains her process and techniques. The teachers offer their own reflections on how they could use and adapt her process for their own teaching situations.

Uses for the Videotape

- If necessary, show one or more of the skits to your children or intergenerational group, following this with the discussion questions and some of the follow-up activities.
- Even better is to use the videotape as a teacher resource — for yourself, your whole faculty, or other groups of teachers and workshop leaders — to see how to do the skits and chants and then do your own work with the children.
- Use the videotape with a parents group, perhaps the parents of children in your group, as a way of demonstrating ahead of time what you plan to do with the children.
- Share the videotape with other educational leaders in your school district or church, or with local cable, PBS, or religious television stations — as a way of encouraging the use of this participatory process as well as consideration of the issues.

How to Order

Each $30 videotape is available in 1/2 inch VHS from the Institute for Peace and Justice or from Meyer-Stone Books.

Guidelines for Participatory Puppetry

The attractiveness of participatory puppetry is in the simplicity and creativity of the process and in the kind of responses it elicits from children. The following guidelines elaborate this process and are all illustrated on both the *Puppets for Peace* and the *Global Family Puppets* videotapes. Viewing this process has been an exciting experience for many teachers and workshop leaders as they come to realize that they, too, can use this participatory process without extensive training or elaborate props.

1. The storytelling process and puppet production are guided by a single leader (teacher, puppeteer, director) who, in effect, stage manages the production while telling the story and involving the unsuspecting audience in the entire process. This person — very likely *you,* the readers of this book — should carry only note cards used for keeping track of the format, story line, and interesting bits of information relating to the artifacts. However, the story is most effectively told without notes.

2. Just before initiating the "show," arrange the artifacts and puppets in front of the seating area. No stage, platform, or backdrop is needed as this is a kind of theater in the round. Because all of the puppets are hand held above head height, it is easy to see the action with groups of 20 to 100.

3. An effective seating pattern is a U shape or horseshoe plan with the audience seated either informally on the floor or on movable chairs. (An auditorium with permanent chairs in rows is not suitable for the kind of informal psychological involvement desired.) The audience should be close to the storyteller and within easy eyesight of the puppets, which are handed out into the group and then brought up to the front of the area.

4. The leader begins to tell the folk tale. One by one the characters are handed out to an unsuspecting "puppeteer" in the audience (often to an adult or child who is not eager to participate). Friendly encouragement is needed to persuade most prospective puppeteers. Simple asides such as "Will you be the Grandfather?" "It's easy," "I'll help you," "A lot of people will be in the story," seem to persuade. The puppeteers and the leader are always in full view of the audience. This in no way, however, detracts from the effectiveness and entertainment value of the puppets.

5. The leader guides everyone through the story and actions, eliciting spontaneous dialogue, if appropriate, and sound effects from the whole audience, if desired. At the conclusion of the tale, the cast of audience puppeteers is lined up and introduced with the appropriate pizzazz. Everyone is applauded. Everyone is thanked for having done an excellent job. Nothing counts as a mistake. In this setting, there is nothing but success. Peers perform and peers reward. The leader congratulates all involved and avoids taking much personal credit. Group success is the reward.

6. Other suggestions: Be creative about what is a puppet and use all kinds of objects (including chil-

dren's arms and hands) and encourage children to design their own materials; involve all the children in some way, even as props (e.g., trees in a forest) and create movement wherever possible (leaves rustling in the breeze); do chants and skits that involve group speaking before doing ones that call for spontaneous insights and problem-solving, because the "safety" of group speaking opportunities seems to lessen children's inhibitions about volunteering to share their own creative thinking later.

Helpful Puppetry Resources

Every public library has numerous books on puppetry. Some of the most helpful puppetry resources for the kinds of simple creative puppets, props, and skits called for in this participatory methodology are illustrated in the following publications from Nancy Renfro Studios, 1117 W. 9th Street, Austin, TX 78703:

Puppetry in Early Childhood Education, by Tamara Hunt and Nancy Renfro. Comprehensive.

A Puppet Corner in Every Library, by Nancy Renfro. Procedures for making puppets and presenting plays and children's workshops.

Pocketful of Puppets: Three Plump Fish and Other Short Stories, by Yvonne Winer, illustrated by Nancy Renfro. Ideas for simple props and stories.

Pocket Full of Puppets: Mother Goose, by Tamara Hunt, illustrated by Nancy Renfro. Simple and creative ways of acting out and illustrating nursery rhymes; adaptable to stories of any kind.

Pocketful of Puppets: Poems for Church School, by Lynn Irving, illustrated by Nancy Renfro. Twenty-four original poems with simple and enjoyable puppet projects.

Part I

PEACEMAKING

THE TRUMPET AND THE MEGAPHONE: AN ARGUMENT!

Theme and Format

This skit uses a dialogue between a trumpet and a megaphone to illustrate that differences often create unnecessary conflicts. Instead, differences can be positive, if each party is willing to view the strengths or gifts of the other as potentially enriching rather than threatening. The skit changes an argument into a search for ways to harmonize differences.

Directions

1. *Materials:* This skit can be done with any "competing" instruments, a toy microphone, a baton, or a piece of paper folded into a megaphone shape. (On the videotape two special instruments are used that were made from cut and welded cotton seed oil cans sent as containers for food for the poor of Brazil from the U.S. government. These cans were converted by rural Brazilians into a kerosene lantern and scoop for selling grain. Because they resemble the shape of a trumpet and a megaphone, they give the skit a global dimension and convey the message that differences can enrich us. The creativity of Brazilian tinsmiths can stimulate our own creative use of scrap material.)

2. Have volunteers share the following dialogue/argument with you:

MEGAPHONE: Now, you listen to me, trumpet, words are a lot better than musical notes. Words are clear, logical, reasonable.

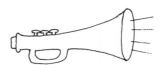

TRUMPET: Music is for the soul, for feeling. I create a mood. I'm better than you are.

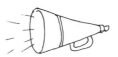

MEGAPHONE: No way! Words are better. Words are good for laws, rules, and thinking!

TRUMPET: But they are so limited. Music is a universal language. Everyone can understand. I can produce happiness.

MEGAPHONE: Words communicate better!

TRUMPET: Words are only good for giving orders! Music moves hearts.

MEGAPHONE: Everyone understands words. Music is confusing and vague.

TRUMPET: Only one person can talk at a time. But music sounds better when many instruments play together...cooperate.

MEGAPHONE: Now that you mention it, maybe we could collaborate and come up with something special.

TRUMPET: Yes! That's it!...we can put together the best of each of us. Both words and music. And if we do, we'll have a...what?

OBSERVERS: A song!

3. Ask the group to identify other "competing" instruments. Examples: a comb and brush; a knife and fork; a shovel and rake; a pencil and crayon; a ruler and compass.

4. Choose pairs. Have each pair of children create an argument and agreeable solution that they can act out. As each pair performs their skit, the onlookers can add suggestions to enrich the drama and extend the "harmonious" solution.

5. Ask the onlookers to figure out additional ways in which the competing members of each pair could work together to create a better situation for all concerned.

Discussion Questions

1. Can you identify some other competing things that make a better whole when combined?

2. Why do people sometimes argue about being better? Why are we sometimes afraid of things that are different?

3. Is there someone who is different from you that you have avoided because of that difference? Do you think there's a way in which that person might enrich you? Is there something you could learn from that person?

4. What are some talents you have that could enrich or help someone else?

5. What are some things that you cannot do well that others could help you with?

Follow-up Activities

1. *Skills sharing:* Children identify a classmate, friend, or family member with whom they can share skills, agree to do a "trade," do it, and share the results with others in the group.

2. *Learning from differences:* Plan an exchange between children who are different (e.g., some with disabilities; some older and some younger; urban children and rural children; children from different religious traditions) and have them share with the group what they learned and how they felt.

3. *Multicultural appreciation:* Have the children name things they recognize and like from cultures other than their own (e.g., Black music; Gospel music; European folk dancing; Mexican or Chinese food) and then some things that they think are peculiar or even threatening (people not speaking English; the way some Asian or Middle Eastern people dress; some Indian, Black, or White hair styles;

some religious symbols). Discuss why some differences seem unattractive, inferior, or even threatening. Brainstorm ways of turning these differences into enriching experiences. Attend a cultural event presented by ethnic groups in your community. Discuss the experience as a group.

4. *Interdependence of countries:* Ask the children to name skills, processes, or resources that we have that can be helpful to other countries and some that other countries have that can be helpful to us.

- Discuss what it means to be "different" and whether "different" means "inferior."
- Ask the children to make up their own story about sharing and cooperating across country boundaries.

Further Resources

1. On conflict resolution, see any one of several excellent elementary teacher's manuals; the first two listed below include interpersonal conflict resolution as well as other levels of conflict and other peace and justice issues:

Conflict Management: A Curriculum for Peacemaking, by Elizabeth Loescher, Cornerstone (940 Emerson Street, Denver, CO 80218), 1984.

Peace-ing It Together, by Pat Fellers (17095 S.W. Eldorado Dr., Tigard, OR 97223), 1981.

Creative Conflict Solving for Kids, by Fran Schmidt and Alice Friedman, Peace Education Foundation (Box 19-1153, Miami Beach, FL 33119), 1983.

See also the resources listed with the following activity, TUG-OF-WAR.

2. On appreciating multicultural differences and counteracting racial stereotypes, see *Educating for Peace and Justice,* vol. 1, units on "Racism" and "Multicultural Education," from the Institute for Peace and Justice; see also all the audio-visual and written resources of the Council on Interracial Books for Children; Camy Condon's *Try on My Shoe: Step into Another Culture* (available from Lynne Jennings, 281 E. Millan Street, Chula Vista, CA 92010); and *Open Minds to Equality,* by Nancy Schniedewind and Ellen Davidson, Prentice-Hall, 1983.

3. Children's books include:

Surviving Fights with Your Brothers and Sisters, by Joy West, Educational Products Division, Word, Inc., 1979. This deals with some of the common reasons why fights occur between siblings and ways for children to deal with them; very well illustrated and interesting for children.

Moja Means One: Swahili Counting Book, by Muriel Feelings, Dial Press, 1974. For young children. An introduction to counting from one to ten in Swahili. The illustrations are exceptional. Both this book and the alphabet book below dispel any stereotypes children have about the fearsomeness of Africa and African people.

Jambo Means Hello: Swahili Alphabet Book, by Muriel Feelings, Dial Press, 1974. For young children. This provides an introduction to Swahili words. The illustrations are outstanding and evoke warmth and dignity.

Let's Talk About Fighting, by Joy Wilt Berry, Children's Press, 1984. This is a book on how quarrels and fights develop. It explores alternatives to fighting.

Why Am I Different? by Norma Simon, illustrated by Dora Leder, Albert Whitman & Co., 1976. Differences in physical make-up, personality, and culture are presented to give children an understanding of others.

2

TUG-OF-WAR

Theme and Format

This poem and skit take a familiar competitive children's game and convert it into a cooperative experience by inviting children to see and feel which they like better—tugs or hugs, i.e., competition or cooperation.

Directions

1. Have two, then three, then four volunteers take the ends of a rope and pretend they are playing "tug-o'-war," or actually play it. If they actually play it, ask the participants how they felt about the game. How did the winner(s) feel? How did the loser(s) feel?

2. Ask for a volunteer to read Shel Silverstein's poem:

HUG-O'-WAR*

I will not play at tug-o'-war.
I'd rather play at hug-o'-war,
Where everyone hugs
Instead of tugs,
Where everyone giggles
And rolls on the rug,
Where everyone kisses,
And everyone grins,
And everyone cuddles,
And everyone wins.

During the reading of the poem, you as leader take a cuddly puppet or stuffed animal and act out the words of the poem—hugging and kissing the volunteers who are holding the rope.

*From *Where the Sidewalk Ends: The Poems and Drawings of Shel Silverstein,* © 1974 by Snake Eye Music Inc., by permission of Harper & Row Publishers, Inc.

3. A further option is to ask the participants to invent some ways of playing "hug-o'-war" that would be in keeping with the words of the poem. Some possibilities:

- players on each end of the rope roll inward until they meet, at which time they hug;

- tie the rope in a circle and invent circle games;
- players see how many times in one minute, for instance, they can roll themselves inward, hug, and then roll themselves back out; they might get three tries to see what their best effort is—working together and competing only against their previous best effort.

Discussion Questions

1. How do you feel when you play "tug-o'-war"?
2. How did you feel when you played "hug-o'-war"?
3. Which is more satisfying?
4. Is it "better" to play games where everyone wins or games where there are both winners and losers?
5. What are the advantages of having everyone win and nobody lose?

Follow-up Activities

1. *Cooperative games:* Before applying the theme of this skit to analogous situations, it might be a good idea to play several cooperative games. Select from sources including:

The Cooperative Sports and Games Book: Challenge Without Competition, by Terry Orlick, Pantheon Books, 1978. This is a wonderful resource of cooperative games, with one chapter devoted specifically to games for pre-schoolers.

The Second Cooperative Sports and Games Book, by Terry Orlick, Pantheon Books, 1982. This sequel to Orlick's first book contains more games from a variety of cultures.

The New Games Book, by Andrew Fluegelman, Doubleday, 1976.

For the Fun of It. Games of cooperation for children and adults, from the Friends Peace Committee, 1515 Cherry St., Philadelphia, PA 19102.

Discuss with the group what makes a game fun. Take a favorite competitive game and invent new rules that make it more cooperative and keep it exciting. (Some cooperative versions of traditionally competitive games can be experienced by children as less exciting.) If you didn't do so earlier, you might go back to "tug-o'-war" and "hug-o'-war" and have participants make up rules for an alternate and enjoyable version of "hug-o'-war."

2. *Other cooperative poems or stories:* Find, or have the children find, other poems or stories expressing cooperation (see "Further Resources" below). Have volunteers act out the poem or dramatize the story.

Have the children write their own poems or stories expressing cooperation and act them out as they are being read aloud.

3. *Analogous situations:*

• Ask the children to identify situations in which they compete with others, situations that seem like "tug-o'-wars" (examples might be competing for the same friend, for grades, for who should be first in line, first to eat, first to get to ride in the front seat), and how they feel in such situations.

• Then ask them to take a tug-o'-war situation and convert it into a hug-o'-war situation; e.g., to get away from competing for grades, someone might suggest having children in various skill areas help those children improve who are not as skilled. Invent a new system of non-competitive "grades."

• For older children, you might extend the analogy to groups and countries, asking the chil-

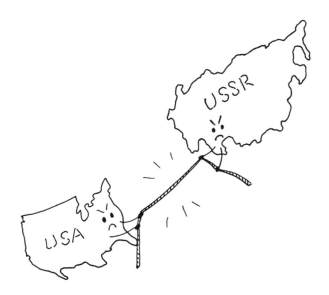

dren to identify ways in which countries play "tug-o'-war" with one another (e.g., over oil and other resources, over votes in the United Nations, over weapons; see TWO FLAGS below, p. 27). Ask them for ways in which these tug-o'-war situations could be converted into hug-o'-war or more cooperative ones.

Further Resources

Children's books include:

Honey, I Love, by Eloise Greenfield, Thomas Y. Crowell, 1978. For young children. Beautiful illustrations, filled with sensitivity and pride, set off this collection. The poems cover a range of experiences, people, and emotions springing directly from a child's everyday life.

The New Games Book, edited by Andrew Fluegelman, Doubleday, 1976. Games for all ages, emphasizing a spirit of fun and cooperation rather than competition.

Where the Sidewalk Ends, by Shel Silverstein, Harper and Row, 1974. Filled with delightful poems and drawings for children.

I'm Glad I'm Me, by Elberta H. Stone, illustrated by Margery W. Brown, G. P. Putnam's Sons, 1971. On building self-concept. A young Black child goes through all kinds of things "he'd like to be" (tree, bird, cloud, etc.) and ends by saying, "I'm glad I'm me." Charcoal illustrations, rich in detail, add a sense of dignity to the story.

I Feel, by George Ancona, E. P. Dutton, 1977. A wide range of emotions are dealt with, and children are allowed to talk about what they see in the pictures and how they feel about them. A good discussion book.

The Sun and the Wind: An Aesop's Fable Retold, by Cornelia Lehn, illustrated by Robert R. Regier, Faith and Life Press, 1983. Lehn has given the reader a beautifully illustrated fable with the sun proving to the wind that love is stronger than force.

Several excellent teacher/parent manuals are:

Friendly Classroom for a Small Planet: A Handbook on Creative Approaches to Living and Problem Solving for Children, by Priscilla Pruntzman, The Children's Creative Response to Conflict Program (P.O. Box 271, Nyack, NY 10960), 1978. Excellent for affirmation exercises, practice activities for teaching creative problem-solving, and conflict resolution ideas. For parents and teachers of preschool and elementary school children.

A Manual on Nonviolence and Children, by Stephanie Judson, Friends Peace Committee, 1977. A wealth of games, techniques, observations, and insights on developing nonviolence in children, especially pre-school and elementary ages.

How to Avoid Word War III at Home, by Elizabeth Loescher, Cornerstone (920 Emerson Street, Denver, CO 80218), 1986. Concrete suggestions about how to handle conflict in the family permeate this book.

Kids Can Cooperate, by Elizabeth Crary, Parenting Press, 1983. Parents and teachers can benefit from the practical activities in this book, all focused on how to encourage children to cooperate.

3

IF YOU'RE ANGRY AND YOU KNOW IT

Theme and Format

This problem-solving chant focuses on creating alternative positive channels for expressions of anger. It affirms the "OK-ness" of feeling anger and the necessity of righteous anger directed at injustice; it invites participants to identify ways of expressing anger that are appropriate and constructive. The example is of interpersonal conflict, but the chant can also be adapted to inter-group or social issue situations, depending on the age of the participants (see Follow-up Activities).

Directions

1. Using the melody of "If you're happy and you know it, clap your hands," teach participants the following first verse:

> If you're angry and you know it,
>
> STOP and think.
>
> If you're angry and you know it,
>
> STOP and think.
>
> If you're angry and you know it,
>
> it's okay for you to show it.
>
> If you're angry and you know it,
>
> STOP and think.

Facial expressions and hand movements:

If you're angry and you know it,

Stop!

and think

It's okay

for you to show it

IF YOU'RE ANGRY AND YOU KNOW IT is adapted from an idea by Linda Williams.

2. Invite participants to make up their own verses and sing them one at a time, again using body movement and expressions as much as possible. Less self-conscious participants can come forward and lead the group offering their own movements as well as new verses. Some could be: "talk it out," "take a walk," "share it all," "say a prayer," "run a mile," "stomp the floor." As leader, you might have to adapt verse suggestions to fit the limits of the song.

Discussion Questions

1. Why is it okay to be angry?
2. What are some good (constructive, healthy, helpful) expressions of anger?
3. What are some bad (destructive, hurtful) expressions of anger?
4. Which of the verses did you think was most helpful or constructive?
5. How do you usually show your anger? Whom do you get mad at?
6. Do you ever get mad at others when you are really mad at yourself?
7. Picture yourself in a likely situation in the near future when you will probably get angry. What would you like to do in that situation after having thought about it today? What can help you remember to act that new way?

Follow-up Activities

1. *Adaptation to inter-group conflict situations:* This chant may be expanded to look at inter-group and international conflict. As such, it could be used in combination with the TWO FLAGS skit (see p. 27 below) by asking what are some ways that two countries show anger at each other? Are there alternatives to military force or other destructive re-sponses? Verses might include the following, but these should not be suggested unless participants are having difficulty identifying their own possibilities: "agree to meet," "talk it out," "get a ref," "go U.N.," "go to court," "use the law," "ask for help."

2. *Adaptation to confrontation with social injustice:* If participants are old enough, the chant can be adapted to an issue of social injustice. Choose a concern, then have the group identify verse possibilities. You may need to give one example to start the process. For example, if the issue is the arms race, some verses might be: "write a letter," "pray for peace," "phone them now," "vote peace in," "tell a friend," "draw my rage," "write a song," "teach a class," "pay no tax."

3. *"Grandfather, Billy, and Lisa":* This simple skit (see p. 14) gives participants the opportunity to act out and develop more fully their alternatives to destructive anger at the three levels of conflict. Any type of puppet (e.g., sock, bag, hand, envelope) can be used. For younger children, you as leader might need to play one of the roles to keep the drama/dialogue going, eliciting further insights from the child participant. Group comment — especially brainstorming alternative scenarios — on each skit is important. Keep the spirit of the interaction cheerful, lively, and supportive. Compliment frequently and stress what is creative and positive.

Surprisingly, this little "puppet show," when enacted spontaneously with parents and children, has the power to stimulate genuine interest in various dimensions of conflict resolution. Interest is heightened by the tiny drama and everyone seems to delight in the chance to use a Lisa or Billy puppet to dream up smart and constructive solutions to the use of anger. Parents and children together can come up with a long list of interesting ways to channel reactions of anger in each of these levels, the home, the community, the country, the world.

GRANDFATHER, BILLY, AND LISA

GRANDFATHER PUPPET: Hmm, well, let's see. Now, Billy, tell me something. What do kids do when they get mad at each other?

BILLY PUPPET (age 8): Kids? Well, they yell or kick or hit or call 'em names. And the big kids fight in gangs sometimes — or throw stuff at each other.

GRANDFATHER PUPPET: And how about the grown-ups? Lisa, what do adults do when they get mad at each other?

LISA PUPPET (age 12): They shout or say bad words or slam the door. Sometimes they ignore each other. A lot of times they get divorced and go away.

GRANDFATHER PUPPET: And what about countries? What do countries do when they get mad at each other?

LISA PUPPET: They get in a war.

BILLY PUPPET: Yeah, they fight with guns and bombs. They call each other names on TV or in the newspaper.

GRANDFATHER PUPPET: So, then, kids, adults, and countries all do the same kinds of things when they are mad. Yep...that's just what happens. So it seems to me we've got to figure out a better way. I bet you two smart kids could help. The getting mad part is okay, but what we do to each other and ourselves just 'cause we're mad isn't very smart or useful. Now you just think for a minute and let's see if we can't figure out something smarter to do for kids or adults or countries when they're really mad. Got any ideas?

---

4. *Specific case studies:* The Discussion Questions already asked participants to focus on specific examples of interpersonal conflict in their own lives. Someone might want to ask the whole group for help with a specific situation. Or the situation might involve inter-group conflict or confrontation with social injustice (see Activities 1 and 2 above).

5. *"Love Your Neighbor":* This chant is a four-part round. The first step is to construct the "puppets,"

using each child's arm and hand. "Did you know you have an instant puppet hanging on the end of your shoulder?"

Ask the group to extend one arm horizontally, then cut it in half with the other hand, raise the forearm and twist the wrist.

Ready!

1, 2, 3...

Cut!

With the four fingers as the roof of the mouth and thumb as the bottom of the mouth, twist the hand ("mouth") around with a squeaking ("rusty") noise and the "puppets" are ready to do their chanting.

*Twist the
mouth around,
SQU-E-E-EK!*

Make the mouth...

The leader can direct this very engaging activity by crisp directions: "Everyone put out an arm. Ready. One, two, three, CUT! One two three, CUT! Twist the mouth around—SQUE-E-E-AK. Open the mouth and say 'Hello.'"

Next, divide the group into four parts and teach each their line before doing the round altogether. The basic rhythm is four "quarter notes" (lines 1 and 4), with line 2 as eight "eighth notes" and line 3 as two "half notes." Emphasis is placed on the first syllable of each line. The first four lines are:

"Love your neighbor"
"Learn to live with one another"
"Friendship"
"Love boom boom boom" (3 heart beats) *

---

*From Grace Nash, *Rhythmic Speech Ensembles,* Nash Publications, 1965, used with permission.

Further Resources

1. See THE TRUMPET AND THE MEGAPHONE, p. 6, for interpersonal conflict resolution resources.

2. On expressing anger (and feelings in general), good children's books include:

The Hating Book, by Charlotte Zolotow, Harper and Row, 1969. The childhood problem of hating one's friend and being devastated by this feeling is presented.

The Quarreling Book, by Charlotte Zolotow, Harper and Row, 1963. A story about people taking out frustrations on each other by picking on the next smaller person.

All the Animals Were Angry, by William Wondriska, Pantheon, 1968. For young children. A dove tells the quarreling animals that she loves them all.

Across Five Aprils, by Irene Hunt, Follett, 1964. For ages 9 and up. For the Creighton family living in Civil War times, there seemed to be no alternative to war, but always war is set in proper perspective, and one sees clearly that no one ever wins a war.

The Story of Ferdinand, by Monro Leaf, Viking Press, 1938. For young children. Classic story of the bull who didn't want to fight.

Let's Be Enemies, by Janice Udry, Scholastic Books, originally Harper and Row, 1961. A story about two little boys with the theme of power struggle. A delightful humorous treatment depicting real child problems that reflect similar adult ones.

What Makes Me Feel This Way? Growing Up with Human Emotions, by Eda LeShan, illustrated by Lisl Weil, Collier Books, 1972. LeShan introduces the concepts of recognizing emotions, identifying the causes for feelings, and finding ways to manage them.

The Hunter and the Animals, by Tomie de Paola, Holiday House, 1981. Presented in stylized detail, this is a wordless story of a forest of peaceful animals who help their enemy, the hunter. He then breaks his gun as an indication that he will no longer try to kill them.

An Outbreak of Peace, by Sarah Pirtle, New Society Publishers, 1987. A young people's art display about peace leads to a plan to enlist an entire New England town in declaring "an outbreak of peace."

4

THE THREE LITTLE PIGS AND THE WOLF

Glove and Finger Puppets

Theme and Format

This chant with a hand or finger puppet has a double theme: conflict resolution and interdependence. The sharing or interdependence theme is twofold. First, there is the sharing between two pigs, one who has food and one who does not. The second sharing is between the pigs and the wolf, representing some person or group quite different from ourselves. In terms of conflict resolution, there is the pig overcoming its fear of the wolf and inviting the wolf to participate. This chant can help children talk about both interpersonal and international conflicts.

Directions

1. *Materials:* Glove, hand, or finger puppets showing three pigs and one wolf. Finger puppets cut out of paper are adequate. The glove puppet used on the videotape has four fringe pom-poms (the type used on curtain tie-backs), three pink with faces of pigs added and one black with the face of the wolf.

2. As you wiggle the appropriate puppet character, have the children recite the chant with you several times:

> This little piggy / had some food.
> This little piggy had none.
> This little piggy / *invited* the wolf.
> [*show surprise*]
> And together they all had some.

3. Ask the children to describe each of the characters in this chant and identify various ways in which this story reflects the reality of their own world and the reality of the larger world. Answers could include:

- The first pig has some food and probably the third pig also, but the second pig doesn't. They represent people in the same group, whether that is a class, a church, a race, a country, etc.

- The wolf may or may not have food but is some person or group the pigs are afraid of (possibly

Copy these faces for glove and finger puppets

a neighborhood bully, a mean school bus driver, a school gang or clique) and some person or group from a different country, racial or cultural background, or age group.

- That they are all attached to the same hand symbolizes their commonality — they are members of the same family and are interdependent.

Discussion Questions

1. In the original "Three Little Pigs" story, why were the pigs afraid of the wolf? Do you think they knew much about the wolf? How did the wolf act? How did the pigs act?

2. Who are the "wolves" in your life? Why are you afraid of them? Do you know much about them?

3. Is there any way that you could reduce your fears and reach out to any of these "wolves" and cease to be enemies or even begin to become friends? Possibilities here might include:

- smiling at a gruff school bus driver and saying "good morning" in a cheerful voice
- talking about a school or neighborhood bully with a teacher or parent, trying to understand why that person might be acting the way he or she does

- praying for one's "wolves"
- if the "wolves" include people from different racial or cultural groups, learning about or meeting people from those groups would help
- if the "wolves" include people from a different neighborhood, then visiting people or places in that neighborhood could help

4. In a Christian religious education context or setting, ask what Jesus' attitudes and practices toward "wolves" would be. Answers should include:

- "Love your enemies."
- "Be good to those who persecute you."
- "Turn the other cheek."
- "Pray for those who persecute you."

5. What are some ways that you are like the first pig, the one who "had some food"? What are some things or skills you have that you could share with others?

6. Are there some ways you are like the second pig?

7. Who are some people you are aware of who are like the second pig who "had none," who do not have some of the things or skills that you have?

8. Are there some ways you could share with one or more of these persons or groups?

tape

Follow-up Activities

1. *"Inviting wolves":* Help the children carry out one of the possibilities they identified in Discussion Question 3 and have them share over a couple of weeks their progress and their feelings about their efforts. Group brainstorming for specific situations where help is desired can provide important peer support.

2. *Sharing with those who "had none":* Have the children follow up one of the possibilities identified in Discussion Question 8 and have them report back to the whole group on how it went, again with the possibility of group brainstorming for situations where help is needed.

3. *Interdependence on a broader scale:* Have the children identify countries who are like the second pig who "had none," resources we have as a country that could be shared with these countries, and ways children could be part of this sharing. Then reverse the situation and have the children identify ways our country lacks certain resources and values that other countries can help provide.

4. *"Sticks and Stones and the Dragon":* As a way of "inviting the wolf" on a global scale, do this longer skit (see p. 39 below).

Further Resources

Children's books include:

The Stranger, by Kjell Ringi, Random House, 1968. For young children. The reactions of a village to a stranger who is so tall his face can't be seen, but who becomes friends with the villagers. Useful for discussing differences between people, enemies, stereotypes, aggression, war, peace, and communication.

John, John Twilliger, by William Wondriska, Holt, Rinehart and Winston, 1966. The message is that dictators are human and reachable as JJ makes friends with the dictatorial mayor and the town changes drastically.

On interdependence, see *Educating for Peace and Justice,* vol. 1, "Mutuality in Education" for application on the interpersonal level, and vol. 2, "Global Interdependence" for application on the international level. On the hunger issue itself, see the unit on "World Hunger" in vol. 2; see also all the resources listed in Part II below.

5

JAPANESE FARM WOMAN

Theme and Format

This reading with a puppet is a true story of a Japanese farm woman who experienced the atom bomb in her city, Hiroshima. It invites participants not only to recall what happened in 1945 but also to identify what they can do today to work with Michiko Fukai for peace.

Directions

Have the children view this reading/skit from the *Puppets for Peace* videotape, or perform it with the children. If the latter, ask for a volunteer to "translate" the Japanese (read the English script — see below). Make a simple puppet by attaching a picture of a Japanese woman to a paper bag puppet or sock. Have the "translator" read the script slowly — line by line — while the puppet acts out the narration. The leader will need to practice once or twice in order to act out the message with simple puppet movements.

JAPANESE FARM WOMAN
(Michiko Fukai, age 60)
"TRANSLATION"

Hello, everyone.
My name is Michiko Fukai.
I am Japanese.
I am from the city of Hiroshima, Japan.
I want to tell you what happened to me on August 6th, 1945.
It was a fine summer day.
The crickets were singing.
I was a young school girl. I loved animals.
Our next door neighbor had a pretty kitten.
I gave it fresh milk.

At 8:15 on August 6th, I went out to feed the kitten.
Suddenly...something *terrible* happened!
Out of the blue sky came a bomb.
It was the first atomic bomb ever used.
It made a bright flash.
The pretty kitten was blinded.
I was badly burned.
More than a hundred thousand people were killed in an instant.
People died of burns even six miles away.
Everything began to catch on fire.
After three hours, the whole city was burning.
Many, many people died.
My mother...my father...and my three sisters were killed.
Every year after that, even today, people in Hiroshima die from the effects of radiation.
Did you know that the nuclear bombs today can multiply the destructive power of that atomic bomb a million times?
We want peace in Japan.
We want peace in the world.
Please work together with me for peace.

Discussion Questions

1. Was this a true story, do you think?
2. What else happened that day in Hiroshima?
3. How did Michiko feel then? How does she feel today?
4. How do you think you would have felt if you had been a child in Hiroshima when the bomb was dropped?

Follow-up Activities

1. *The story of Sadako Sasaki:* Present this story of another victim of the bombing of Hiroshima,

Sadako Sasaki, who died of leukemia in 1955 because of the radiation from the bomb; she was two years old in Hiroshima when it was bombed. Before she died, she tried to fold a thousand origami paper cranes as a prayer for recovery and peace. She made only 644, but her Japanese classmates finished the thousand and children all over the world continue to make paper cranes, many of which hang on a special monument to Sadako in Hiroshima Peace Park. The story can be shared in several ways:

- *Sadako and the Thousand Paper Cranes,* a book by Eleanor Coerr, is available from the Fellowship of Reconciliation (P.O. Box 271, Nyack, NY 10960) for 4th–6th grade readers.

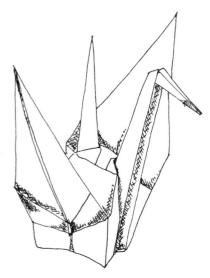

- A 20-minute readers theater version (dramatic reading) is printed in *Families Peace-ing It Together,* an intergenerational workshop models guidebook for leaders, forthcoming from the Institute for Peace and Justice and Meyer-Stone Books.
- A filmstrip entitled *Creating Peace in Our Lives* includes Sadako's story as a major theme; available from Twenty-Third Publications, P.O. Box 180, Mystic, CT 06355.

2. *For junior high children and older, show a Hiroshima film:* The gruesome images of burn victims and death that are included in films like *The Last Epidemic* (testimony from Physicians for Social Responsibility and available from Impact Productions, 1725B Seabright, Santa Cruz, CA 95062) and to some extent in a book like *Hiroshima no Pica* are generally too emotionally overwhelming for younger children and thus we discourage their use below junior high. The film *Bombs Will Make the Rainbow Break* (a documentary on the Children's Campaign for Nuclear Disarmament, from Films, Inc., 1213 Wilmette Ave., Wilmette, IL 60091) contains some of these images in children's drawings but also focuses on what children are doing for peace right now. Such resources help children to realize that it is not an impersonal "enemy" that is killed in war, especially in nuclear war. It is people — children, grandparents, friends — who are killed.

3. *Other peacemakers:* This skit or PEACE SOUP provide an opportunity to focus on specific peace persons and peace actions. Have children find local examples as well as more famous peacemakers. The unit on "Today's Peacemakers" in *Educating for Peace and Justice,* vol. 3, lists children's books and AV's on seventeen famous, mostly contemporary, peacemakers. Cornelia Lehn's *Peace Be with You,* Faith and Life Press, 1980, presents the stories of historical peacemakers, many but not all of whom are famous. Invite the children to make a list of all the things they learned that people can do for peace.

4. *What can we do for peace?:* Have the children focus, finally, on the invitation from Michiko Fukai: "Please work together with me for peace." Ask the children to brainstorm a list of all that *children* can do for peace. Invite them to choose one of the possibilities as their own next step for peace and consider a class or group action for peace.

Further Resources

Let Peace Begin with Me, by Mary Lou Kownacki, Twenty-Third Publications (P.O. Box 180, Mystic, CT 06355), is a five-lesson unit on children as peacemakers for 4th–6th grades in a religious education setting; the story of Sadako is a central focus and the making of paper cranes is one of the activities.

Children's books include:

Hiroshima no Pica, by Toshi Maruki, Lothrop, Lee & Shepard, 1982. For middle grades. A poignant story of the effects of the bombing on one family.

A Jar of Dreams (and other books) by Yoshiko Uchida, Atheneum, 1981. Set in the Depression, this book gives a positive view of what it means to be a Japanese American and dispels stereotypes about this ethnic group.

- Make each crease as exact and as firm as possible.
- Don't give up! It might take more than one try to complete a successful crane!

Folded Paper Crane

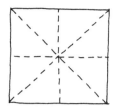

1. *Use a perfectly square piece of paper; make 4 exact creases; unfold after making each crease.*

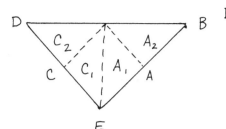 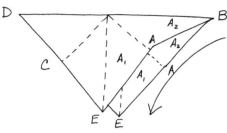

2. *Fold on a diagonal crease. Face point E toward you. Lift side A at point A and tuck section A2 inside section A1, bringing point B inside and down to point E.*

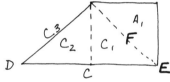

3. *Repeat with side C. Lift side C at point C and tuck section C2 inside section C1, bringing point D inside and down to point E. Crease C3 folds down inside vertically along center line F of the diamond (see Figure 4).*

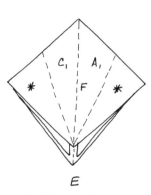

4. *Keep open end of diamond (point E) facing down. Fold top outside halves (*) of sides A1 and C1 along the dotted lines to center line F. Turn over and repeat, so that all points meet at open end (point E) and you have a kite-shaped figure.*

5. *Fold top section G back and forth over the front and back, making a firm crease along the dotted line.*

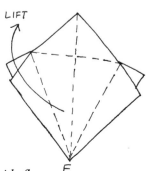

6. *Unfold the four side flaps; lift the top flap up from point E to form a canoe-like figure (see Figure 7).*

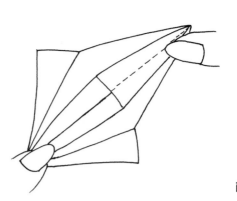

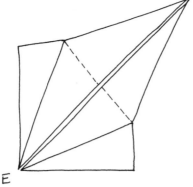

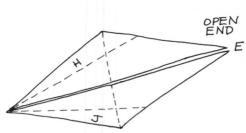

OPEN
END

E

8. Working on the sides
   opposite the open end (point E),
   fold flaps H and J to center.
   Turn over and repeat.

7. Flatten down the long sides along existing creases,
   so that the long sides touch in the middle.
   Turn over and repeat, lifting again from point E.

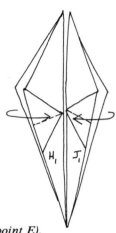

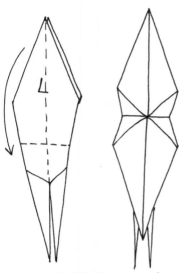

9. Holding the figure
   with the open end up (point E),
   fold the front two halves (H1 and J1) together.
   Turn over and repeat.

10. Fold front top half L down over the narrow points
    (the crane's legs) so that the underside creases
    all meet at the center. Turn over
    and fold the other top half down to the same line.

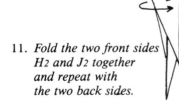

11. Fold the two front sides
    H2 and J2 together
    and repeat with
    the two back sides.

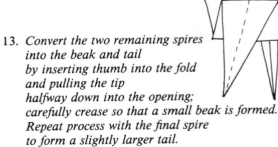

13. Convert the two remaining spires
    into the beak and tail
    by inserting thumb into the fold
    and pulling the tip
    halfway down into the opening;
    carefully crease so that a small beak is formed.
    Repeat process with the final spire
    to form a slightly larger tail.

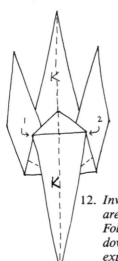

12. Invert, so that all points
    are facing up.
    Fold upper two-thirds of wing K
    down to points 1 and 2,
    exposing a small triangle
    at the center of the crane.
    Turn around and fold down
    the other side in the same way.

14. To make your crane stand up, turn it upside down,
    spread the wings about 1 inch and blow hard into the hole
    under the belly so that the body puffs up.

6

FRIENDS AND ENEMIES

Theme and Format

This short history lesson helps us see how quickly friends and enemies have changed places during the last forty or fifty years. In relationship to the United States, four major countries — Japan, (West) Germany, China, and Russia — have changed from the category of "friend" or "enemy." Participants may consider the possibility of Russians and other "enemies" once again becoming "friends." Changing country relationships is contrasted to losing all life in a nuclear war.

Directions

1. *Materials:*

• a yardstick

• two pieces of cloth about twelve inches wide, with FRIEND written on one and ENEMY on the other

• four clothespins to attach each cloth to the stick

• four signs attached to clothespins with each bearing the name of one of the four countries: CHINA, JAPAN, GERMANY, RUSSIA

2. Two volunteers are asked to hold the stick. Explain that the skit is an illustration of recent history showing how countries can be our friends at some times and then enemies and how things can change even in one lifetime.

3. Wave the FRIEND cloth as in a handkerchief greeting or farewell to a friend and then hang it at one end of the stick. Wave the ENEMY cloth at one side using it in a bull-fighting-like action suggesting

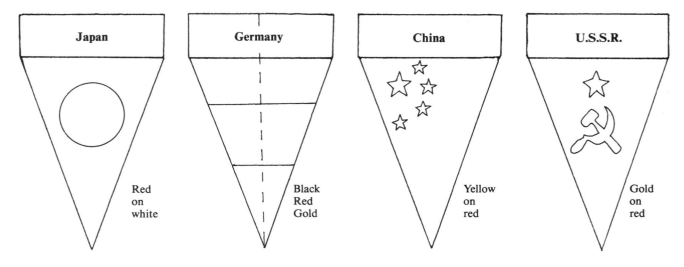

Flags for "Friends and Enemies" Skit

23

conflict and then pin it to the opposite end of the stick. Pick up the JAPAN card and ask the participants:

> "Fifty years ago, JAPAN was _____"
> [*have them say "an Enemy"*].

Attach the card to the stick above the ENEMY cloth. Proceed to the others:

> "Fifty years ago, GERMANY was _____"
> [*an Enemy*].
> "Fifty years ago, RUSSIA was _____"
> [*a Friend*].
> "Forty years ago, CHINA was _____"
> [*an Enemy*].

4. Then update (that is, reverse) the relationships, by asking the participants:

> "Today, JAPAN is _____" [*a Friend*].
> "Today, GERMANY is _____"
> [*half Friend, half Enemy.*]
> "Today, RUSSIA is _____"[*an Enemy*].
> "Today, CHINA is _____" [*a Friend*].

5. Give the final line:

> "Friends come and go, even in one lifetime, but life once lost is lost forever. Nuclear war with one enemy means losing all life. No more friends. No more enemies. Let's learn how to love our enemies."

6. Place the final version of the stick in some central place, have the volunteer holders return to their seats, and go to the discussion questions.

Discussion Questions

1. Why were each of these countries "friends" or "enemies" fifty years ago (forty for China)?
2. Why do these countries change from being friends or enemies? Who decides?
3. Could they change again?
4. Why is Russia considered an "enemy" today? Why was China an "enemy" and now is a "friend"?
5. What kinds of things could help change Russia from being an "enemy" into being a "friend"? Answers to this might include:

- meeting Russian people or having a Russian pen-pal
- learning more about Russian people today
- learning more about Russian history and culture (music, dance, festivals, food)
- praying for friendship and peace
- exchanging students, teachers, clergy
- having political leaders meet and talk more often
- reducing fear by agreeing to limit and reduce the nuclear arms race
- cooperating on joint space, scientific, and cultural projects
- learning each other's language

6. Which of these activities can children do?

Follow-up Activities

1. *Implement answers to Discussion Question 6:*

- Pen-pals: for linking with a Russian pen-pal, children ages 7–15 can send their letters to "Kids Meeting Kids Can Make a Difference," Box 8H, 380 Riverside Drive, New York, NY 10025.

- Pictures: a poster and postcards of Russian children and adults for classroom or home are available from the Fellowship of Reconciliation, Box 271, Nyack, NY 10960.
- Flags: put flags of Russia and the U.S. (from a UNICEF store) in the classroom or home as a symbol of our desire for peace and friendship and as a reminder to pray for peace and friendship.
- Reading: find story books about Russian people; show children copies of *Soviet Life* magazine (a *Life* magazine-style publication written in English by Russian authors and available from the U.S.S.R. Embassy, 1706 18th St., NW, Washington, DC 20009), which provides pictures as well as interesting information; there are features on the U.S.S.R. in back issues of *National Geographic* magazine.
- Cultural events: attend a Russian movie, ballet, or art exhibit.

2. *"Bread and Salt"**: The Russian word for hospitality is *"Khleb"* (bread) *"sol"* (salt). Together the words mean entertaining and welcoming with bread and salt. When bread is offered, the guest is honored. A lavish Russian meal will have several delicious loaves of bread.

In olden times in Russia, it was a custom to give a guest a beautiful loaf of freshly baked bread and a wooden dish of salt. The guest was then invited to cut the first slice of bread and dip it into the salt while saying, "Khleb da sol" (bread and salt). Sharing bread and salt became a symbol of hospitality and is still practiced today in some homes.

3. *Peace poems:* Have the children recite the following poem from a Russian schoolgirl and share their feelings and thoughts about its content. Then invite them to compose their own poems for Russian schoolchildren. These could be sent along with letters to Russian pen-pals (see Activity 1 above).

---

*Adapted from Darra Goldstein, *A la russe: Cookbook of Russian Hospitality.*

I WANT TO LIVE

I want to live and not to die.
I want to love and not to cry.
I want to feel the summer sun,
I want to sing when life is fun.
I want to fly into the blue,
I want to swim as fishes do.
I want to stretch out friendly hands to all
    the young throughout the land.
I want to fight for what is right
    against deceit — against despair —
    against hunger everywhere.
I want to live — I want to live!
No atom bomb annihilate my shining world!
I want to love and not to cry —
I want to live and not to die.

The author of this poem, a young girl, recited it in English and then in Georgian to a group of Americans visiting School 53 in Tbilisi in April 1984.

4. *Pantomime Russian proverbs:* Using the techniques of charades, have children act out several or all of the following Russian proverbs, one at a time. Discuss the meaning of each before going to the next one. For younger children, simplify some of the words.

- It is easier to take the sword from the wall than to hang it back again.
- Distrust is an ax at the tree of love.
- One peace is better than two wars.
- If you are afraid enough, you'll believe that the earthworm is St. George's dragon.
- There is always time to do good.

5. *Pairing U.S. and Russian cities:* A group called Ground Zero (P.O. Box 19049, Portland, OR 97219; tel.: 503-245-3519) has matched U.S. cities with Russian cities with comparable populations and similar economic characteristics and provides information on how U.S. cities can organize some kind of exchange on either a large or small scale. Some communities have made this an official city-wide effort. In other communities, a single church or other community group has done this as a very limited exchange. They gather pictures, letters, articles, artifacts, etc., that portray their community and send the box to their Russian "sister" city. Children could play major roles in one of these efforts.

Further Resources

See *Educating for Peace and Justice,* vol. 2, "The Relationship between the US and the USSR," for additional suggestions, especially for older children, and for background reading for your own preparation.

Children's books include:

The Peace Book, by Bernard Benson, Bantam Books, 1982. A tale about a small boy who, hearing about nuclear death and destruction, contrives to appear on television to say that he is just a small boy who doesn't wish to die because of the decision of a handful of world leaders. He becomes famous and is summoned to meet with heads of state who explain that they don't dare to disarm because they don't trust each other. All seems lost until the boy comes up with an ingenious solution.

Wacky and His Fiddlejig, Stanford Summers (484 W. 43rd, Apt. 24-0, New York, NY 10036), 1980. Dedicated to the children of the Third World, the story concerns one of Santa's helpers who finds himself out of step with his co-workers in the military toy department. Finally he decides to quit, preferring to spend his time creating a toy that will appeal to a child's imagination.

The Butter Battle Book, by Dr. Seuss and A. S. Geisel, Random House, 1984. About an "arms race" between the Zooks and the Yooks. This is a wonderful way for children to talk about escalating conflicts and about who is "the enemy."

7

TWO FLAGS

Theme and Format

This simple pantomime uses two small flags as a visual interpretation of U.S.-Soviet relations and how they might proceed in the years ahead. It asks the children to identify each stage of the relationship and provides an opportunity to have them identify ways of helping toward a positive conclusion. (There are many interpretations of the action, but often it is seen as a metaphor for the nuclear arms race.)

Directions

1. Ask two volunteers to hold your mini-stage (consisting of a rope over which is draped some kind of material, e.g., a blanket or bedspread) while you as leader operate behind or below the stage with the U.S. flag and the Russian flag (generally available wherever UNICEF materials are sold). Hiding in back of a chair works just as well.

2. Present the following sequence of movements:

A: Blow on each flag one at a time at center stage (independence).

B: March each flag one at a time across the stage (superpower assertion of power).

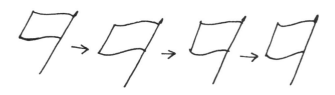

C:

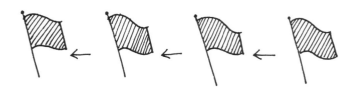

D: Have the two flags march together and clash at center stage (confrontation).

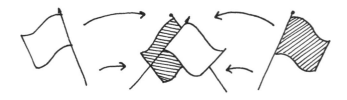

E: Have them point and jiggle each other angrily.

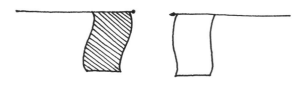

27

F: Have the two escalate upwards above the stage, with the U.S. generally going higher first and the Russian flag catching up (the arms race primarily, but suggesting other forms of competition as well).

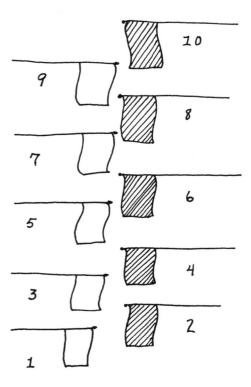

H: Approach to friendship — slowly move the two toward each other, crossing over each other, crossing back, touching (becoming friends).

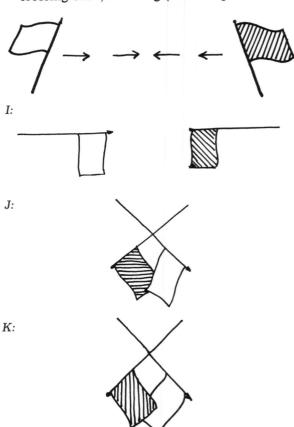

I:

J:

K:

L: Blow the two flags together (mutual respect, equality, cooperation).

G: At the limit of your upward stretching (escalating), have the two flags collapse and flop over the stage at separate ends (exhaustion of resources, economic collapse).

3. Ask the children to explain each stage of the sequence, repeating the movements as you focus on each stage. There isn't necessarily only one "right" answer or interpretation, so affirm a variety of responses. Another possibility is to have the children

make their own paper flags and act out the skit themselves.

Discussion Questions

1. If you are not going to use FRIENDS AND ENEMIES as a way to consider how to help make the Russians friends instead of enemies, then you might deal with that issue here, using the Discussion Questions in the FRIENDS AND ENEMIES skit.

2. What are some of the ways the U.S. and the U.S.S.R. have been trying to be better (the "escalation" or "arms race" stage) than each other? Answers might include: in gaining allies, supportive votes in the UN, selling arms to other countries, getting the most raw materials like oil, Olympic medals, as well as being ahead in the arms race.

3. Why do you think either country would want to be ahead in the arms race?

4. Do you think it does any good to be ahead? What happens when more than one wants to be ahead?

Follow-up Activities

1. *Reversing the arms race:* Because PEACE SOUP, JAPANESE FARM WOMAN, and FRIENDS AND ENEMIES all provide opportunities for children to identify ways they can work for peace, you might not want to do this follow-up activity but instead proceed to one of them for the action dimension. However, because this skit provides the opportunity to deal directly with the nuclear arms race itself, you might want to focus your action concerns on just that issue at this time. If so, here are some suggestions:

- ask the children to draw pictures of the arms race coming to a halt or turning around; you might entitle the drawings: "freezing the arms race."

(The Institute for Peace and Justice conducted a local/national "Art Peace" effort with such a focus and has instructions for similar efforts.)

- show the children (7- to 11-year-olds) the videotape production of *Buster and Me,* a 20-minute Mr. Rogers-style muppet show (from Impact Productions, 1725B Seabright, Santa Cruz, CA 95062). Three muppet children hear about the arms race, get scared, are helped by adults to understand what's happening, and then discover what they can do to work for peace. At the end they ask viewers to help them do more.

- invite the children to share their feelings about *Buster and Me*—whether they have ever been afraid of nuclear war, had a nightmare about it, felt excited about playing war, felt scared or good about taking action, felt hopeless.

- have children respond to the actions of Buster and his friends: Were they good things to do? Could they be done by ourselves as well? Which ones would they like to do, either individually or as a group? What other possibilities are there for children to work to reverse the arms race?

- for older children (ages 11–13) there is a 20-minute 16mm film entitled *Bombs Will Make the Rainbow Break* (from Films, Inc., 1213 Wilmette Ave., Wilmette, IL 60091) on children's nuclear fears, the madness of the arms race, and many ways that children are actually working to reverse the arms race. You might consider inviting someone from the Nuclear Freeze Campaign to explain their proposals for "freezing" and reversing the arms race and how children might participate.

2. *"The Arms Race":* This is a 10-minute participatory relay race developed by and available from Camy Condon (235 Mezcal Circle, N.W., Albuquerque, NM 87105). It shows the history of the arms race by having two children, one representing the U.S. and the other the U.S.S.R., race forward carrying the date each country developed a particular weapon system. The U.S. is ahead ten times and the U.S.S.R. three. For 10–13 year olds.

Further Resources

See FRIENDS AND ENEMIES above, p. 23.

8

PEACE SOUP

Theme and Format

This skit asks participants to call out the key ingredients in peacemaking and can thus focus on both the interpersonal and international levels of conflict resolution. It can serve as a short "summary" of many of the preceding skits and chants or as the opportunity to discuss and decide on specific actions children can do for peace.

Directions

1. Using any puppet (a cook with a large soup spoon is the most appropriate), announce to the children that you are making "peace soup." They ask "pea soup?" "No," you say, "peace soup!" If they ask again, "pea soup?" you answer louder, "No, peace soup!" The audience finally says, "Oh, peace soup!"

2. The cook puppet asks for some of the ingredients for "peace soup" and with each answer says "one cupful of . . . [whatever ingredient is voiced]" — love, listening, forgiveness, sharing, praying, marching, hugs, etc. If you think one or more are especially appropriate, you could say "two cupful of" that ingredient.

3. After filling the "pot" with these ingredients, have your hand puppet stir the peace soup and declare: "Peace is delicious!" Then everyone pretends to slurp up a big spoonful saying, "Peace is delicious!"

Discussion Questions

1. Which of the ingredients do you think are the most important?

2. Which of the ingredients would be the easiest for you to do?

3. Which would be the hardest?

4. What are some other ingredients for making peace in your home? in our class? in the world?

5. If your "peace soup" were made up of people, who would you put in your soup?

Follow-up Activities

1. *"Pocketful of Peacemakers"*: Using Discussion Question 5 and an apron with large pockets and finger puppets or photos on a stick to represent various peacemakers, have the children identify historical and contemporary peacemakers. Each child can learn something about their "favorite" peacemaker and make a hand or finger puppet representing that peacemaker. See the seventeen peacemakers and resources in the unit "Today's Peacemakers" in *Educating for Peace and Justice,* vol. 3, and Cornelia Lehn, *Peace Be with You,* Faith and Life Press, 1980.

2. *Making peace soup at home:* Encourage each child to ask the other members of their family if they would like to "make peace soup" at home. Direc-

tions and discussion questions will be similar to the above. You can duplicate them and send them home with each child, explaining to the parents the activity and goals. Encourage each family to identify one or two ingredients they would like to concentrate on as a family or have each family member choose one that they will personally concentrate on. This could be spread over several weeks or months, with new or "improved" ingredients selected each time (e.g., weekly, monthly).

3. *"World Peace Soup":* This can be either a group project or individual actions or both. Ask the children to identify one thing they could do for "world peace soup"; when they've done that, ask them to share the results and their feelings. Again, this can also be a family project. Examples of children's peace actions are given in FRIENDS AND ENEMIES and TWO FLAGS above. Additional projects include:

- Children's Campaign for Nuclear Disarmament (CCND, RD 1, Box 346, Chadds Ford, PA 19317) has organized a letter-writing campaign to the president of the U.S. each year since 1980, with representatives bringing these letters to the White House and reading many of them publicly. See the film *Bombs Will Make the Rainbow Break* describing this campaign (see TWO FLAGS above).

- Poems or essays on peace written for a creative writing class can be sent to national political representatives, as can art projects on peace.

- Classes or a school can have a peace award as part of a larger assembly honoring children who have excelled in various areas.

- Children could check their local toy store for "G.I. Joe" items and other war toys and write the manufacturers if any of them feel these toys are inappropriate. They might also contact Sue Spencer (205 E. Leeland Heights Blvd., Lehigh Acres, FL 33936) about "Toys for Peace," a non-profit organization she is forming, and tell toy manufacturers about the kind of "peace toys" they would like to see provided.

Further Resources

Families Acting for Peace is a 6-page pamphlet detailing numerous action suggestions for making peace in the home, some initial steps in family action for world peace, and some more challenging steps for whole families. Available from the Institute for Peace and Justice (1–9 copies: 50 cents each; 10–99: 25 cents each; 100 or more: 20 cents each).

Peacemaking for Children is a bi-monthly activity sheet for children published by Jackie Haessly (2437 N. Grant Blvd., Milwaukee, WI 53210) offering peacemaking activities on both the international and interpersonal levels.

The Parenting for Peace and Justice Network (PPJN) Newsletter includes specific children's peacemaking activities and a variety of resources for use with children, as well as whole family peacemaking suggestions. Contact the PPJN at 4144 Lindell Blvd., #122, St. Louis, MO 63108, for further information on the PPJN and its bi-monthly newsletter.

Children's books include:

Children as Teachers of Peace, edited by Gerald Jampolske, Celestial Arts (231 Adrian Road, Millbrae, CA 94030), 1982. A book of drawings, poems, letters to world leaders on peace by children; "a book written for adults by kids! Because the simplest thoughts are sometimes the best."

My Shalom, My Peace, edited by Jacob Zim, McGraw-Hill – Sabra Books, 1975. A moving collection of paintings and poems on the theme of peace, by Arab and Jewish children.

Rain of Fire, by Marion Bauer, Clarion Books, 1983. For grades 5 and up. An anti-war story about two brothers, their feelings about World War II and Hiroshima. 1984 Jane Addams Peace Association Award Book.

The Fragile Flag, by Jane Langton, Harper & Row, 1984. For grades 5 and up. The story of children who organize grassroots, nonviolent resistance to the nuclear arms race.

Ain't Gonna Study War No More, by Milton Meltzer, Harper & Row, 1985. For grades 8–adult. An extraordinary important service to the cause of peace is made by this history of civil disobedience. It illuminates the theories, thoughts, and deeds of generations of heroes who bravely rejected all violence, or participation in particular wars they considered unjust.

Strands of thousands of origami paper cranes were made in Iiyama City, Japan, by Japanese students. Author Camy Condon holds up the cranes to tell the story of "Sadako and the Thousand Paper Cranes" (see p. 19).

9

WALKING GALLERY

Theme and Format

Visualizing the results of active peacemaking is the goal of this art project. Children imagine "How Peace Looks"...and color or paint their images. Holes are punched in the top two corners of the completed portraits, which are then hung with bright ribbons around the necks of the artists—children who carry their vision on parade around the room, school, community center, church, or neighborhood.

Directions

1. *Materials:*

- drawing paper
- crayons
- colored markers or paints
- ribbon (about 12" per child)

2. Ask the children to "imagine what peace looks like." Close your eyes and say the word "Peace." Sing a song or play music that sounds peaceful. When the children have an image, they should draw or paint their idea of peace.

Because many children have vague or passive images of peace—they are much more concrete about their images of war—one alternative is to ask them to image peace *as a verb*. What would it mean to "do peace"? What would it mean or look like for someone to be "peace-ing."

3. When the peace picture is completed, it should be hung around the child's neck as a moving portrait. When everyone is ready a parade can happen with the walking gallery carried around the room—out into the school, church, community center or even a shopping mall. Children should be encouraged to describe their art to admirers.

Follow-up Activities, Further Resources

See PEACE SOUP above, p. 30.

10

BRICK WALL

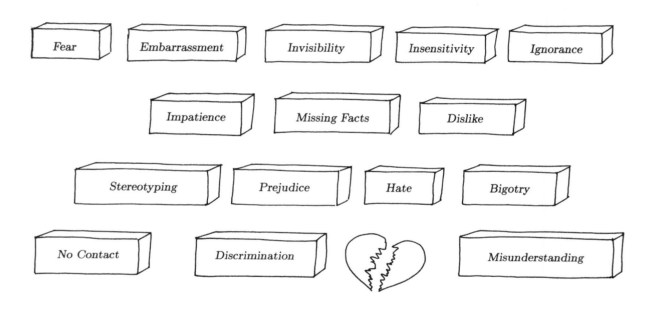

Theme and Format

This skit demonstrates how our negative attitudes build brick walls separating us from other people. The group helps the leader find examples of each attitude in the experiences of people in the audience. The skit concludes with all holding up their hands and symbolically breaking down the brick wall barriers, symbolizing a change of heart. Brick-wall barriers are built against race (racism), age (ageism), sex (sexism), and against people who have physical, cultural, mental, or language disabilities.

Directions

1. Make fifteen paper bricks (cover with clear contact plastic for repeated use) with one word printed on each brick. Each is a negative attitude:

Dislike	Embarrassment	Stereotype
Fear	Insensitivity	Misunderstanding
Prejudice	Ignorance	Discrimination
Hate	No Contact	Missing Facts
Impatience	Invisibility	Bigotry

2. Make one large red paper heart. Cut it in half with a jagged cut.

3. Use a hand puppet as leader and pointer. Select a volunteer to use the puppet.

4. Ask eight volunteers to stand up in front of the group. Give each volunteer two cardboard bricks to hold. Gather all the bricks together in a way that they touch and form a two- or three-layer wall. (You can also pass the bricks around in a circle.)

5. Whisper to the puppeteer to walk back and forth near the wall, bumping dramatically against the bricks four or five times, acting dazed and bumping again.

6. Announce to everyone that this is the brick wall made up of the negative attitudes we each carry in our hearts.

7. Have the puppet leader bump into each brick one at a time. After the bump, the audience reads the brick name out loud, and the puppet asks, "What does it mean? When did you feel this? Can you think of a time when this brick got in your way or was a barrier to others?"

8. After all (or most) of the bricks have been illustrated with life examples, the puppet asks everyone to put their hands up and, on the count of three, break down the walls in their hearts. One, two, three... everyone pushes in the direction of the brick wall and the bricks are tossed up in the air to fall in a scattered mess around the room.

9. The puppet concludes with the sentence, "We can break down the barriers we build to keep others away everyday. Let's start today."

Follow-up Activities

1. *Positive Alternatives:* Each child holding a brick barrier can be invited to name one or two ways his or her particular brick barrier could be overcome. For example, the brick of fear might be overcome by getting to know something about the person or group feared or by asking a friend to go with you to the person, place, or situation that is the object of fear.

2. *Making enemies into friends:* See the Follow-up Activities in FRIENDS AND ENEMIES above, p. 23.

Further Resources

Educating for Peace and Justice: National Dimensions has a wide range of classroom activities and action suggestions on racism, ageism, handicapism, sexism, and other barriers to human interaction and interdependence.

11

WAR-TOYS-R-US

Theme and Format

This movement of baby clothes, shoes, and war toys to the music of "We Are the World" represents young life gradually being replaced by choices of death. Its simplicity is emotionally powerful, but the message of hope is also clear. We have a choice. We can make a better world for ourselves. We are the children who can open our eyes and help change the direction from death toward life.

Directions

It is best to practice this skit once or twice before performing it before a group. It may be done by one to four people.

1. *Materials:*

- a record or tape of the song "We Are the World"
- a long table
- 2 chairs
- a clothesline

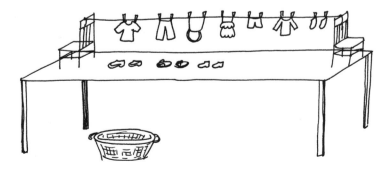

- 12 clothespins
- a clothes basket
- 8 war toys (for example, jet fighter plane, tank, helicopter, little gun, big gun, submarine, rocket and missile, soldiers)
- 8 used baby clothes, including a bib
- 3 pairs of used baby and young children shoes

2. Ahead of time, put the two chairs on top of the table at each end and stretch the clothesline between them.

3. Fold the baby clothes and arrange them on one side of the bottom of the basket. Put the war toys in the basket on the other side and the three pairs of shoes on top of the toys. Place the clothespins next to the clothes.

4. Introduce the skit and begin the song (record or tape). The performer walks through the audience carrying the clothes basket up to the front and stands in front of the table in the middle of the clothesline area. One by one, the baby clothes are taken out and hung on the line. The performer should look happy and the action is a familiar laundry scene. The baby clothes should hang across the whole line. (A baby bib is especially effective right in the middle.) This should take about one-third of the song time.

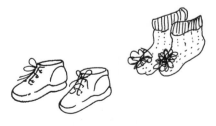

5. Next, the performer picks up the first pair of baby shoes (baby booties or white walker shoes are good) and puts one on the fingers of each hand. The

36

shoes are walked across the table right under the clothesline from one end to the other in an action that looks like a baby walking. Take them off and leave them together on the table at one end.

6. Repeat this action with the second pair of shoes. Walk, skip, and dance the shoes under the hanging clothes and leave them next to the first pair at one end of the table.

7. Repeat with the same type of actions and leave the shoes next to the other shoes. By this time the song should be two-thirds over.

8. Now remove a clothespin and take off one item of clothing. Reach into the basket and lift a war toy out, pretend to play with it in the air, then place it under the missing clothes. Take off another item and replace it with a war toy. Do this until all of the clothes are off the line and the war toys are lined up on the front of the table.

9. Replace each pair of shoes by a handful of toy soldiers or a larger militaristic doll.

10. As the song concludes (timing is crucial) the performer should bend down and pick up the basket, which now holds the clothes, shoes, and clothespins and walk out through the middle of the audience group.

11. The war toys are left under the empty clothesline.

Discussion Questions

1. How did the music make you feel?
2. How did you feel at the end?
3. Describe what happened in the pantomime?
4. What did it mean to you? (Note: The action is somewhat ambiguous. There are many possible interpretations; no one is more correct. Some see the larger issue of increased government spending for weapons making less available for human needs, represented by the baby's clothes. Others see more kids playing with war toys these days and fewer kids playing with things like dolls. Still others see an allegory on war — the toy symbols of deadly weapons kill children, the first casualties in real war.)
5. Do you think war toys are okay?
6. Why do many people think they are bad?
7. If you agree that they are bad, what can you do? What can we all do together?

Follow-Up Activities

1. Organize a parent-teacher meeting on the subject, preceded with some materials sent home to the parents (see Further Resources below).

2. Have students bring in any war toys they have for a group discussion about whether any of them are okay.

3. Have the children, with their parent(s), watch one or several of the new TV cartoons that have been created by the toy manufacturers specifically to sell their toys of violence. Discuss what they saw.

4. Have a "turn in your war toys" day at which students bring in the war toys they are willing to let go of forever. This could be done as a ceremony, perhaps including elements of worship.

5. "Just saying no" is not usually enough for children. They need to experience alternatives that are equally exciting. Such experiences could range from students bringing in examples of their own exciting alternative toys, to a toy fair at which local toy merchants or manufacturers display their creative alternatives.

6. Discuss with the children the possibility of declaring their classroom or the whole school a "war toys free zone." A number of pre-schools and day care centers have made such a declaration. Encourage the children to discuss this idea with their family and consider a similar declaration by the family about their home. Cards are available from Donnelly/Colt (see below) for such declarations.

7. Bumper stickers, stuffed animals, buttons, and small stickers, all focusing on opposition to war toys, are available from Donnelly/Colt, Box 188, Hampton, CT 06247. Peace Links distributes a wonderful "Peace Pal" bunny who holds the whole world in her hands. Write them at Peace Links, 747 8th St., S.E., Washington, DC 20003. The 9-inch high bunny comes with a brochure explaining the bunny's origin, with ideas on alternatives to war toys.

8. Encourage the children to write individual, family, group, or class letters to Coleco (makers of the G.I. Joe toys) and other war toy manufacturers, explaining their concern about war toys and the need for alternatives.

9. Many nationally known cartoonists have created cartoons specifically criticizing war toys. Get and show examples to the children. After discussing them, invite the children to create their own cartoons either criticizing war toys or promoting alternatives. For sample cartoons and other suggestions, contact the cartoonist who started the whole effort: Bob Staake, 1507 Lanvale, St. Louis, MO 63122; tel.: 314-961-2303.

Further Resources

1. The June 1987 issue of the newsletter of the Parenting for Peace and Justice Network (4144 Lindell Blvd., St. Louis, MO 63108) focuses on this issue. Also available from the Network is a 4-page pamphlet on "War Toys and Christmas" from Alternatives (Box 429, Ellenwood, GA 30049).

2. "Parents Guide to Non-Violent Toy Buying" is a twenty-five-page pamphlet published by the Board of Church and Society of the United Methodist Church. It contains information and ideas about children's play, toys, and TV violence, and also lists toys to avoid and sources of toys with possible play value. Excellent and inexpensive, the pamphlet sells for $1.00 from Discipleship Resources, P.O. Box 189, Nashville, TN 37202. Order number CS116.

3. *Kid's America* and *The Toy Book,* both by Steve Caney, give children and those who work with children hundreds of toys to make with household materials. These books contain lots of imaginative and educational ideas.

4. *The Toy Chest,* by Stevanne Auerback, is a source-book of toys for children; it is designed to help parents choose toys appropriate to a child's growth and needs. It is available from Lyle Stuart, Inc., P.O. Box 3204, Burbank, CA; tel.: 913-504-0204.

5. For more information on toys and alternatives to toys, write to the Toy Project, c/o Dee Dee Arledge, at the Libra Foundation, 3308 Kemp, Wichita Falls, TX 76308.

6. Toys for Peace is an association that develops alternative toys. Write to Sue Spencer, 205 E. Leeland Heights Blvd., Lehigh Acres, FL 33936.

12

STICKS AND STONES AND THE DRAGON

Theme and Format

This skit is a short allegory (15 or 20 minutes) on the arms race, and it can be used to illustrate any escalating conflict. It is most appropriate for older children (8 to 13-year-olds).

Directions

See PRODUCTION SUGGESTIONS below. Following the script there are ideas on puppet construction.

Discussion Questions

See the questions posed by the NARRATOR near the end of the script. Once these questions have been discussed and the skit concluded, then you can go to the following additional questions:

1. Why were the villagers afraid of the dragon?

2. What kept them from fighting each time they threatened each other?

3. Do you think the lamb was right or do you think it was dumb? Why?

4. Are there situations in the world today like this one? Are there some "lambs" too? Who?

Follow-up Activities

1. See all the options in THE THREE LITTLE PIGS AND THE WOLF, FRIENDS AND ENEMIES, TWO FLAGS, and PEACE SOUP.

2. Help children imagine the "conversion" of weapons factories and technologies to peaceful production by having them draw pictures of what peaceful new products and services could be made there. School science fair projects can focus on this theme of peace conversion.

Further Resources

1. See all those listed with THREE LITTLE PIGS AND THE WOLF, FRIENDS AND ENEMIES, and PEACE SOUP.

2. *If* is the title of a 5-minute 16mm cartoon showing the conversion of nuclear weapons production and transportation to life-supporting and life-enhancing situations. It uses no language, only marvelous images, and is appropriate for all ages. Available from the United Nations Association, 300 E. 42nd Street, New York, NY 10017.

Puppet Characters

DRAGON (may be played in three parts: head, tail, and fire)
VILLAGERS:
    Stone Carrier – Villager 1
    Stick Carrier – Villager 2
    Knife Carrier – Villager 3
    Gun Carrier – Villager 4
    Missile Carrier – Villager 5
LAMB
NARRATOR (adult reader, director, stage manager, story teller)

Production Suggestions

No stage is necessary. The audience can be seated in a half circle with the children on the floor in front. The puppeteer/performers may be selected spontaneously from the assembled group as the story unfolds. The audience plays the part of the village voices.

The narrator acts as a stage manager and guides all the participants through their lines and actions. Only the narrator needs to be familiar with the script and read from a copy. The adult whispers the lines to the players. Another method is to invite readers from the audience to read the script from the front of the room while the puppeteers perform the actions.

Note: Children invited to this play may bring their favorite toys or stuffed animals and use them as the villagers in the story.

STICKS AND STONES
AND THE DRAGON

NARRATOR: Once upon a time, a virtuous, courageous, and honorable dragon lived in the midst of auspicious clouds of multiple hues on the top of a mountain. The dragon could breathe FIRE!

DRAGON: WOOSH...ROAR...WOOSH...ROAR!

[*The audience may dramatize the fire with swaying arms and repeating loud "wooshing" sounds.*]

NARRATOR: Of course, it was not known that the dragon was virtuous, courageous, and honorable. The only thing the people in the village below the mountain knew about the dragon was that it was "different" and it could breathe fire.

DRAGON: WOOSH...ROAR...WOOSH...ROAR!

NARRATOR: Also, because the villagers had seen cartoons of dragons on TV, they knew some of the common stereotypes of dragons. They were supposed to have teeth like a tiger, scales like a fish, a mane like a lion, feathers like a bird, and eyes like humans. [NARRATOR *points to any girl in the audience.*] The smartest girl in the class had read in a book that "in ancient China dragons could command the elements. They were related to the sun god." One of the boys [*points to a boy*] knew that dragons were often pictured with a pearl of knowledge in their forked tongues.

DRAGON: WOOSH...ROAR...WOOSH...ROAR!

NARRATOR: For years all the people of the village [*points to the audience*] ignored the presence of the dragon. [*Instructs the audience to turn their heads away from the dragon.*] But gradually hostilities increased in what was called a "cold war." [*Instructs the audience to shiver.*] They began to speak.

[NARRATOR *tells sections of the audience to call out as the cold war mentality builds.*]

AUDIENCE:
A: We don't like that dragon up there!
B: It's different. I'm afraid of it.

C: Maybe it will use its fire on us and attack us first!
D: That fire is dangerous. We need shelters!
A: All dragons are bad. 'Ya seen one, ya seen 'em all.

NARRATOR: One villager decides to take action.

VILLAGER 1 [*with stone*]: I'm going up on that mountain. I'm not afraid.

AUDIENCE: Wow! You're brave!

VILLAGER 1: Hey, dragon! Better watch out! I'm gonna get you. I've got this big stone, and you've had it!

DRAGON: Hi, there. What's the matter? Why do you have that big stone?

VILLAGER 1: 'Cause the people of the village are afraid of you. You're dangerous! You're different! You're a dragon!

DRAGON: Sure I'm a dragon. My mother was a dragon, too.

VILLAGER 1: Well, you've got fire!

DRAGON: WOOSH...ROAR...WOOSH...ROAR! Well, I use my fire only when I'm threatened...when I'm afraid, ya know. And to keep me warm in the winter.

VILLAGER 1: Everybody's afraid of you, so I'm going to knock your head off!

DRAGON: Gee, if you do that, I'll have to blow you away. I don't want to be stoned!

NARRATOR: The villager and the dragon stare at each other menacingly, eyeball to eyeball, but in the end they back away choosing not to use violence.

VILLAGER 1: I guess I'll let you go this time. But you better watch out the next time.

NARRATOR: The villager returns to the people and everyone says:

AUDIENCE: You're terrific! [*cheers and applause*]

NARRATOR: Everything is calm for awhile, but after a time, a second villager decides to take action.

VILLAGER 2 [*with stick*]: I'm going up on that mountain. I'm gonna get that dragon and teach it a lesson.

AUDIENCE: Wow! You're brave!

VILLAGER 2: Hey, dragon! Better watch out! I'm gonna get you! I've got this big stick!

DRAGON: A big stick? What do you have a big stick for?

VILLAGER 2: Well, all the people of the village are afraid of you. You're dangerous and different. You've got fire!

DRAGON: WOOSH...ROAR...WOOSH...ROAR! You're right, it is fire. But I only use my fire when I'm afraid. And I use it a little in the winter to keep me warm.

NARRATOR: The villager and the dragon stare at each other, eyeball to eyeball, but both prefer non-violence so they back away.

DRAGON: I guess I'll let you go this time.

VILLAGER 2: Okay, but you better watch out next time.

[AUDIENCE *cheers.*]

NARRATOR: Then another villager stands up.

VILLAGER 3 [*with knife*]: Hey, everybody. Look what I've got. A knife! I'm not afraid. I'm going up that mountain.

AUDIENCE: Wow! You're brave!

VILLAGER 3: Hello, dragon! I've got to protect my people. I'm going to get you. I've got a knife!

DRAGON: I'm getting worried. Maybe I'm going to have to build up my fire power. Why do you have that knife?

VILLAGER 3: Our village isn't safe. We've got to build up our national defense. We're afraid of you!

DRAGON: Gulp...I'm afraid of you, too. Maybe I can try for a bigger ROAR...WOOSH!

NARRATOR: Again the villager and the dragon confront each other, eyeball to eyeball, but finally back away from violence.

VILLAGER 3: I guess I'll let you go this time. But you better watch out.

[AUDIENCE *cheers the return of Villager 3.*]

NARRATOR: The village people were quite happy for awhile, but then winter came and hard times affected their lives. Once again they turned against the dragon.

[NARRATOR *instructs sections of the audience to call out:*]

AUDIENCE:
   A: We better build up our defenses.
   B: It'll make more jobs if we build things like guns and missiles.
   C: We have to protect ourselves.

NARRATOR: And so they took up a collection. Everyone gave taxes, about 50 percent of each week's allowance. Some of the people began to complain but everyone paid for the new weapons.

VILLAGER 4 [*with gun*]: Okay. I'm ready now. We built this big gun. Now I'm going up on that mountain and take care of the dragon. I'm not afraid.

AUDIENCE: Wow! You're brave!

VILLAGER 4: Hey, dragon, you better watch out! I've got a big gun! I'm gonna protect the village and fight fire with fire!

DRAGON: A gun? That's terrible. I'm going to have to think of something powerful, too. It's tough keeping up with you in this arms race.

VILLAGER 4: We gotta look out for our own interests. We gotta protect our families and our way of life. You better watch out!

NARRATOR: The villager and the dragon stare at each other, eyeball to eyeball, but both prefer non-violence so they back away.

VILLAGER 4 and the DRAGON [*speaking together*]: Well, I'll let you go this time. But the next time you better be careful.

[AUDIENCE *cheers the return of Villager 4.*]

NARRATOR: The researchers, scientists, and builders of the weapons had new ideas. They made plans and they began to speak out.

[NARRATOR *instructs a small group in the back to whisper together and then call out:*]

AUDIENCE:
   A: We need lots of money for new and more accurate weapons.
   B: We've got something terrific.
   C: It's a brand new missile! An experiment.
   D: We're dying to find out if it works.

VILLAGER 5 [*with missile*]: Everybody here has to give up half their allowance AND lunch money for three years. I'll take up a collection so we can get this missile off the ground.

AUDIENCE [*many groan and protest*]:
A: Oh, no... not more money.
B: That's great, but it sure is expensive. Do we have to give up our lunch money *and* our allowance?
C [*small group in back*]: Sure, you want to protect your country, don't you?
A: We gotta have the newest stuff!
B: We gotta protect our way of life!

VILLAGER 5: Thanks. Check this out, a missile! The biggest thing we've ever built. We could make a hundred of 'em, and put a lot of bombs on the tip, right here. I'm not afraid. I'm going up and get that dragon.

DRAGON: All that powerful stuff against me!

VILLAGER 5: It's a Big "M" Missile! See right up here on the tip. It's got ten hydrogen bombs. It's the newest thing... and it's got 99 percent kill probability. You better watch out, dragon. This thing won't work unless I use it to get you *first*.

DRAGON: You mean you've got first-strike capability?

VILLAGER 5: You said it... I didn't. We might even make one hundred of these missiles: that's one thousand nuclear bombs!

DRAGON: Oh, no, that's terrible! I still remember when a lot of dragons in my family were killed the last time there was a war. I'm just gonna have to keep up this race with more firepower on my side.

NARRATOR: The two of them begin to stare eyeball to eyeball, on the brink of disaster, when suddenly a little lamb from the village appears and speaks up.

LAMB: Hi! Mind if I lie down over here, next to the lion, er, the dragon? We have to stop all this. I think everyone is having the wool pulled over their eyes. No allowance, no lunch money! The people of the village are being fleeced! And we're all in terrible danger.

AUDIENCE [*Various people and groups call out*]:
A: Look at that lamb! No weapons, defenseless.
B: You're gonna upset the balance of power!

C: You're going to ruin our deterrence!
A: What's that little lamb chop doing?
B: It looks like a lamb in lamb's clothing!

DRAGON: Maybe the lamb is right. I just thought of something. If you get me with all these bombs on your missile, this whole mountain will be ruined.

VILLAGER 5: I think I see what you mean. If the mountain is destroyed, it will fall down on the village and instead of protecting ourselves, well, we would be destroyed too. I never thought of that.

LAMB: Good. That's just what we need to do; start thinking, start talking, and start cooperating. We gotta get together and stop threatening the whole world with total destruction because *nobody* wants that.

AUDIENCE:
A: I think the lamb is right.
B: We should think about the consequences of this violence.
C: Yeah, but what about our jobs? We make money building those bombs.

LAMB: Everybody's got a right to have a piece of the PEACE and a piece of the job action, too. We need a conversion of our military industry, and we need people with your talents to figure out peaceful life-enhancing work for you missile builders.

AUDIENCE:
A: When ya think about it, it's a good idea.
B: We don't want those bombs to blow up the mountain and have all the fallout come down and hit us.
C: A lot of people would be killed or sick. And their kids would be sick.
A: The birds and animals would be blinded.
B: And nothing would grow. Anybody left would starve.
ALL: They're right. We all need a piece of the PEACE.

DRAGON: I kinda like the idea of peace, too. Then I wouldn't have to be afraid of you and you wouldn't be afraid of me.

VILLAGER 5: It sounds great. But what are we going to do about this peace conversion?

DRAGON: There's just one thing. I've got this natural fire inside me, something like a volcano. And it's my only talent. If I stop blowing fire I won't have anything to do.

LAMB: Together we have a lot of talent and resources. Let's ask the villagers to help us think of what to do....Do you have any bright ideas out there?

[NARRATOR *can now elicit ideas from the whole audience as to how to end the story. The "ideas" prop can be a light bulb. Pass it around and ask for suggestions as to how the dragon and the villagers could cooperate peacefully. How could the bomb and missile makers be constructively employed and how could the natural talents of the dragon benefit the village? The ending of the puppet play may be made up spontaneously with these solutions. A suggested conclusion is as follows:*]

LAMB: Let's see if we can piece together this problem. The dragon has a natural talent for using fire, and it's important that he has something to do to keep his self-respect.

AUDIENCE:

A: Maybe we could get him to convert his natural fire [*passes the light bulb*].

B: Yeah, how about using those clouds? We could use the fire to make steam and the steam could heat our houses all winter long.

C: Some of our experts could work on solar energy, too, instead of missiles. Maybe we could help the whole world make use of free sunlight to stay warm and cook and drive solar cars. We could help a lot of people with that kind of technology.

D: We could build a big pipe from the dragon's mountain down to our houses and the steam from the clouds could supply all our energy needs.

DRAGON: That's a great idea! I'll bet that a couple of my natural puffs and roars and wooshes would make enough steam-generated energy to go into every house in the village.

LAMB: Let's go! The Fire Conversion Steam Energy project will begin!

[NARRATOR *asks the audience to pretend hammering and building vigorously.*]

NARRATOR: It was a fine plan. Everyone helped with the project. The dragon roared and wooshed three times a day and everybody benefited. The dragon felt pride in being employed and was respected by the whole village. The talents of everyone were turned to peaceful projects that helped even the villagers far away. The dragon was honored by the Girl Scouts and his story was featured on the six o'clock TV news.

Even today, right here in your city, people have a place of honor for the dragon's natural fire. Maybe you've got one in you're own home. It's called a "FIREPLACE." It's a place for sitting around, a place for keeping warm, a place for keeping the PEACE.

THE END

ASSEMBLY SUGGESTIONS FOR PUPPETS

Copy figures. Attach to cardboard. Laminate or cover with clear contact paper for durability. Attach arms and legs to body with brass paper brads. Attach puppet to popsicle stick or chopstick with tape.

Villager 1: Stone Carrier

Villager 2: Stick Carrier

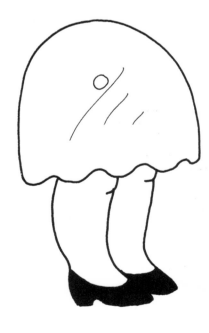

Villager 3: Knife Carrier

Villager 4: Gun Carrier

Villager 5: Missile Carrier

OPTIONAL FINGER PUPPETS

*Cut out figures, bend to fit finger,
and attach with tape.*

Two young volunteers help to demonstrate that relationships between countries, like relationships between people, can change from "friend" to "enemy" and "enemy" to "friend" *(see p. 23).*

The audience demonstrates how negative attitudes can build a "brick wall" between individuals *(see p. 34).*

Part II

GLOBAL AWARENESS

13

THE WORLD IN A BASKET

Theme and Format

We are all one family everywhere on earth. A variety of objects, puppets, or dolls from various countries are handed out to the audience and everyone is invited to identify which country each comes from.

Directions

1. Have a basketful of puppets and/or dolls or paper dolls from different countries. UNICEF puts out a set of paper dolls from around the world. Ask the children to identify the country of origin.

2. International paper dolls: Cut out pictures of people from different countries from old issues of the *National Geographic* magazine. Paste on cardboard and glue on an ice cream stick.

3. Invite everyone to bring in from home any doll, or other special toy or souvenir, from another country or culture. Put these in a basket and distribute them to the group, inviting each child to say something about the item and guess the country it came from.

4. Sing together a song like, "We've Got the Whole World in Our Hands...," using as the variation each time a different group of people—e.g., "We've got the people of China in our hands..." or "We've got our friends in Mexico in our hands...." A globe could be passed from child to child as the song is sung.

Discussion Questions

1. What are some of the things that make us similar to people from other countries?
2. What are some of the things that make us different?
3. What are some of the ways that you feel like a global family? Who is your brother or sister in another country?
4. What does it mean to sing, "*We've* got the whole world in our hands"? How do we have other people or the whole world in our hands? How do our choices affect others far away?

Follow-up Activities

1. *Country research:* Ask each child to report on the country his or her puppet or doll or picture came from (Direction 2 above) or choose a country from among the puppets or dolls you brought in. Focus the report on what it's like to be a child in that country (see BREAD/RICE FOR THE WORLD, page 56 below, for Japan).

2. *Discovering global connections:*

- Ask the children to identify things they use that come from other countries, starting with their toys, clothes, bikes (even if the finished product is from their own country, some of the raw materials—e.g., petroleum for making plastic—come from other countries).

- Have the children check their food pantry and refrigerator at home and make a list of those food items that came—in whole or in part—from other countries.

- Ask children to think of ways their family, church, community group (e.g., Girl Scouts and Boy Scouts), or whole city is linked with people of other countries. Examples could include relatives living abroad, church missionaries, residents traveling abroad, trade or other business relationships abroad, foreign students at a local high school or college, foreign doctors at a local hospital, visiting entertainment or cultural groups, and foreign films.

3. *Living interdependently:* Ask the children to identify one way in which they can each live out the words of the song "We've Got the Whole World in Our Hands." Examples could include prayer, sharing resources (food or dollar collection for the hungry), pen-pals. See the five final skits in Part I above and 100 HUNGRY PEOPLE and THE RABBIT IN THE MOON below for many other possibilities.

4. *"Globalize" your classroom:* Invite the children to list ways of making your classroom more visually representative of the global family. This might include a world map, a globe, a "world heroes" bulletin board on which pictures and articles about famous people from other countries are displayed (rotating weekly or monthly), a shelf or display of books and magazines from or about other countries.

5. *"Global Celebrations":* Celebrate holidays and other days of importance to various cultures. Combine this with studying a different culture each month. Use art, music, clothes, and displays for that month's culture.

Further Resources

The United Nations Association (300 E. 42nd St., New York, NY 10017) and its local chapters and the U.S. Committee for UNICEF (331 E. 38th St., New York, NY 10016) have a wealth of resources for teachers and parents on the global family, global interdependence, and children from around the world.

Educating for Peace and Justice: Global Dimensions (Institute for Peace and Justice) contains several units on global interdependence and peace that offer a wide variety of classroom activities for elementary teachers and action suggestions for elementary children.

For children's books, see pp. 73 below.

SOME DAYS TO CELEBRATE

UNICEF's *Festival Book* (U.S. Committee for UNICEF, 1966) describes festivals celebrated by children in different countries; for young readers. Similarly, *Days to Celebrate,* by Ruth Allen Miller (Jane Addams Peace Association, WILPF), presents special days with suggestions for celebrating them; the book includes some folklore, biography, and background for many unusual holidays. The festivals described in UNICEF's *Festival Book* are:

NEW YEAR "TET"	Vietnam	January or February
NEW YEAR	Ethiopia	September 11
NEW YEAR "PHI MAY"	Laos	Mid-April
DIVALI (Hindu Festival of Lights)	India	November 9
NOW-RUZ (New Year)	Iran	March 21
HANNAKUH (Jewish Feast of Lights)	Israel	Mid-December
DOLL FESTIVAL	Japan	Early March
POSADAS	Mexico	December 16–24
SINTERKLAAS (St. Nicholas)	Netherlands	December 5–6
END OF RAMADAN (Moslem Breaking of the Fast)	Pakistan	Spring
EASTER	Poland	Spring
LUCIA DAY (Feast of St. Lucy)	Sweden	December 13
SONGKRAN (Buddhist New Year)	Thailand	April 13–15
HALLOWEEN	U.S., Canada	October 31

The best recent source for how to celebrate these and other holidays is the *To Celebrate* edition of the *Alternative Celebration Catalogue* (Alternatives, P.O. Box 429, Ellenwood, GA 30049).

14

EAT WITH A SPOON

Theme and Format

This chant helps us think about ways different people meet basic human needs. It raises the question about whether "different" means better or worse, proper or improper. The intent is to enable children to see differences as enriching and to discover that each culture has customs and manners (in this case, table manners) that guide children to be polite and act appropriately in their own cultural setting.

Directions

1. *Materials:*

- spoon
- fork
- chop sticks

2. Teach your children this rhythmic chant and have them say it with you several times, using appropriate actions to simulate the various eating options:

> Eat with a spoon – Slurp, slurp
> Eat with a fork – Crunch, crunch
> Eat with your fingers – Yum, yum
> Eat with chopsticks – Nibble, gulp

Discussion Questions

1. Where do people live who eat with spoons? forks? fingers? chopsticks?
2. What are some rules or manners connected with eating with a spoon? a fork? your fingers? chopsticks? What seems natural to you? What seems funny or odd to you?
3. What are some other activities that people do differently in different cultures (greetings, dances, songs)?

4. Does "different" mean better than your way? or strange and worse than your way? What does "different" mean to you?
5. What might seem odd about your table manners or dress to someone visiting from a different culture?
6. In what ways are all people the same?

Follow-up Activities

1. *Appreciating one's own culture:* Have the students name one thing (or as many as possible) that makes them feel good about their racial, cultural, or religious heritage. Example: I feel good about being Puerto Rican (or French, or Korean, or Black) because...
2. *Visuals for commonalities and differences:* In order to help children get a better grasp of the commonalities among people, discuss with them some of the ways in which people are similar. Using visuals (older students might want to prepare a slide show) is one way. For example, show pictures of people in families, caring for children, playing, praying, telling folk tales, or legends. Visuals can also be used to make the concept of differences more concrete, always with the intention of helping children see differences as enriching. Music and other art forms can be used to emphasize the point that people express themselves artistically in different ways, and that all of these ways are good.
3. *Speaker from another culture:* Invite someone from another culture or country to share some aspect of their traditional home life with your children. Make sure the discussion includes identifying ways we all can be enriched by each other's cultures. Invite speakers to teach one or two words of greeting or a short song in their native language.
4. *Identifying and challenging cultural and racial stereotypes:* Show the class pictures of people from

various racial and ethnic groups. Have them write a story about one person. Discuss whether or not stereotypes enter into their story. Ask them to explain why they developed the story the way they did. A few simple questions may aid the children in developing their story, e.g.: Where does this person live? Where does this person work? How does he or she dress? What does he or she do for recreation?

Set up situations, learning activities, reading assignments, guest speakers, field trips, visual displays that will directly counter stereotypes. *For young children,* one possibility to counter the racial stereotypes connected with physical appearance is to make paper dolls by cutting photos from magazines or pictures and pasting them on cardboard. Draw or cut out various types of clothing for the dolls. Some could be traditional dress, others can be "modern" dress. So, for example, a Navajo doll could have one type of outfit to wear for a ceremonial dance and another to wear at work or at home. *For middle-grade children,* through the use of pictures, show them that all Asian people do not look alike.

The filmstrips from the Council on Interracial Books for Children (1841 Broadway, New York, NY 10023) are excellent, especially *Unlearning Indian Stereotypes, Unlearning Asian American Stereotypes,* and *Unlearning Chicano and Puerto Rican Stereotypes.*

Further Resources

On appreciating multicultural differences, see *Educating for Peace and Justice,* vol. 1, units on "Racism" and "Multicultural Education" (available from the Institute for Peace and Justice); all the audio-visual and written resources of the Council on Interracial Books for Children; Camy Condon's *Try on My Shoe: Step into Another Culture* (available from Lynne Jennings, 281 E. Millan St., Chula Vista, CA 92010); and *Open Minds to Equality,* by Nancy Schniedewind and Ellen Davidson, Prentice-Hall, 1983.

15

BREAD/RICE FOR THE WORLD

Theme and Format

This chant focuses on cultural differences, inviting children to appreciate and learn from such differences. While the specific difference is food, the application can be broadened to many other cultural differences.

Directions

Note: The Discussion Questions and Follow-up Activities below are fewer than with EAT WITH A SPOON, p. 54, and TRY ON MY SHOE, p. 58, because each of these chants has a similar theme. Most of the activities could be done with any of the chants. We have put most of them with the other two chants, with the exception of two, both of which are most appropriate here.

1. *Materials:* none is essential, but a rice bowl and a pair of chopsticks make the activity visually more interesting.

2. Do the chant in a way similar to EAT WITH A SPOON but also as a three-part round, each part naming a different meal time (Dinner, Lunch, Breakfast):

> Rice for dinner,
> Rice for dinner.
> Isn't it nice
> that you and I
> Both — like — rice.

You can pantomime eating rice with chopsticks while singing the round.

Discussion Questions

1. Name some places where people eat rice for breakfast and lunch as well as dinner.

2. Where in your country is rice grown? Are there different kinds of rice?

3. What kinds of rice dishes do you like?

4. Can you think of celebrations, festivals, or holidays in which rice (or corn) plays a special role in the celebration?

Follow-up Activities

1. *Prepare a special rice dish:* This could be a joint class project, or the children can each bring in a different rice dish that they enjoy. One West African dish is from Ghana:

JOLOFF RICE WITH MEAT OR CHICKEN

- 2 lbs. of beef or 1/2 lb. of chicken cut in pieces
- 1 8-oz. can of tomato sauce
- 1 large onion, chopped
- cooking oil
- 1/8 cup butter or margarine
- 2 cups of rice
- salt and pepper, to taste
- water
- red pepper (optional)

Cut meat or chicken into pieces. Fry in hot oil. When brown, add one cup of water, onions, tomato sauce, and red pepper. Allow the stew to simmer until the meat is almost tender, adding more water as necessary. Add rice, water, and salt according to package directions. Boil for about 10 minutes, reduce heat, and simmer until all of the water has boiled away and the rice is done. Toss with butter and salt and pepper. Serves 6 to 8.

An excellent source for a wide variety of dishes from other countries is a children's cookbook entitled *Many Hands Cooking: International Cookbook for Girls and Boys,* by Terry Touff Cooper and Marilyn Ratner, Thomas Y. Crowell Co.

2. *"My Perceptions of Japanese People":* This activity for middle-grade and middle-high children asks a number of questions to help children identify their attitudes about Japanese people. You can put the following questions on a worksheet for each child (you may want to adapt the language depending on the age of your children):

- "When I think of Japanese people, I think of..."
- "If I went to Japan, I would expect to see..."
- "Some Japanese foods are..."
- "Three adjectives that describe the Japanese are..."
- "Three Japanese cities are..."
- "The greatest similarity between people in Japan and in the U.S. (or Canada) is..."
- "Some Japanese words I know are..."

After they have completed these statements, record the answers on pieces of newsprint or on a blackboard. This is a way for all to see what others in the class think about Japanese people. Discussion should focus on the sources and the accuracy of the perceptions. You could ask how strong an influence each of the following sources has been in these perceptions: books, magazines, newspapers, TV, movies, home, school, friends, other. Discuss Japanese heritage in this country and talk about ethnic Japanese living in your own community.

16

TRY ON MY SHOE

Theme and Format

This chant focuses not only on appreciating cultural differences but also on seeing things from different points of view. It invites children to make personal as well as intercultural or international applications by theoretically "walking in another person's shoes." We hope to literally and figuratively "try on other cultures" by means of shoes, hats, and clothing.

Directions

1. *Materials:* None is essential, but an interesting shoe from another culture would be helpful.
2. Teach everyone the following lines:

> Try on my shoe.
> It's as good as new.
> It fits! It fits!
>
> Go where I go.
> Know what I know.
> It fits! It fits!
>
> See what I see.
> Understand me!

3. *Optional:* Do a similar chant with hats:

> Try on a hat.
> Now what about that!
> It fits! It fits!
>
> Go where I go.
> Know what I know.
> It fits! It fits!
>
> See what I see.
> Understand me!

4. *Leader reflections:* You might want to add these reflections after the Discussion Questions or in conjunction with the Follow-up Activities: "If we try on someone else's shoe or walk in another person's footsteps, if we understand that we have sisters and brothers all over the world and learn to think about other peoples' points of view, maybe we can work more effectively on some of the injustices, like hunger, that we have seen in this program."

Discussion Questions

1. Have you ever learned something special from a person from another culture?
2. What are some ways of experiencing customs of people from other cultures?
3. Do you know any words from another language? Or a song in another language?
4. Did you ever try to see something from another's point of view (e.g., your parents, a brother or sister, someone you disagreed with, another country)?
5. Think of a time when you felt misunderstood. Explain how you felt. How could a friend have helped by "being in your shoes"?

Follow-up Activities

1. *Appreciating cultural differences:*

- go to a local cultural festival
- learn a song from another culture
- listen to a record from another culture
- see a movie in another language
- play a game from another culture
- eat a dish or meal from another culture (see BREAD/RICE FOR THE WORLD above, p. 56)

- read a children's book in another language (for children's books, see below p. 73)
- celebrate holidays from other cultures (UNICEF books are a good resource; see also the list on p. 53)

2. *Seeing things from another's point of view:*

- Perhaps using puppets, invite children to role play conflict situations in which they take the opposite side of the position they had in the actual situation, as a way of experiencing another's point of view.

- Have children exchange an extra shoe for a day, so that each is carrying around another's shoe and is asked to try to see things that day from the point of view of that person. The children can report to one another what their shoe experienced that day and some of their attempts to see things from that person's point of view.

- It might be easier for some children to practice such a skill in less personal situations first. THE TRUMPET AND THE MEGAPHONE, p. 6, and THE THREE LITTLE PIGS AND THE WOLF, p. 16, are two possibilities.

- STICKS AND STONES AND THE DRAGON, p. 39, applies this crucial principle of conflict resolution to the international level, although children could also discuss it in terms of their own fears.

Further Resources

Try On My Shoe, by Camy Condon, is the title of a 72-page book on multicultural puppetry (see details below, p. 63).

For children's books, see p. 73 below.

An "argument" between two instruments serves to illustrate ways of "harmonizing" our differences (see p. 6).

Young students are fascinated by an intriguing stick puppet from another part of the world.

17

THE RABBIT IN THE MOON

Theme and Format

This Japanese folktale skit invites children to consider sacrificial sharing. The willingness of the rabbit to give its life for the old man does not imply that children should copy the rabbit literally, but rather identify ways they can give of themselves for others.

Directions

1. *Materials:*

- an "old" man puppet (perhaps a paper bag puppet or a paper plate puppet)
- a chair for the old man to stand on
- several animal puppets, including a rabbit
- a transparent scarf to suggest the moon (if possible)

Paper plate

dering and playing with one another.] Then the old man said: "I wonder...which animal is the kindest animal in the world?"

He jumped down out of the moon, turned himself into a beggar, and walked into the forest saying, "I'm hungry. I'm so hungry."

When all the animals heard the old man, they said together: "Let's help the old man." They talked among themselves and decided to go out and look for some good things to eat. [*Send them out looking for imaginary food.*] The old man waited patiently and then the animals all returned [*have them sit down in a row opposite the old man*].

Then they said: "*Konnichi wa* [good afternoon]. I found you something delicious to eat. I found you some _____ [*name a fruit or vegetable*]."

To this the old man replied: "*Arigato* [thank you]." [*The animal could add: "Do you like fresh strawberries, old man?" and the old man could respond: "I love fresh strawberries." Send each animal back to its place with a sentence like: "The monkey was very pleased to be able to help the old man."*]

The rabbit was the last animal to come forward. When it was the rabbit's turn, it came up to the old man, crying [*have the puppeteer cry profusely*].

The old man said: "What's the matter?"

But the rabbit kept crying [*have the puppeteer pretend to cry even more loudly*].

2. Find volunteers for each puppet as you tell the folktale. When the puppets speak to one another, whisper the lines in short segments and have them repeat each segment. Ad-libbing and flexibility should be encouraged rather than sticking to an exact script. The folktale goes as follows:

THE RABBIT IN THE MOON

The story begins with an old man who lived in the moon [*have the volunteer stand on the chair and cover the old man puppet with a transparent scarf*]. One day he looked down on the earth and saw a beautiful forest [*tell all the children to sway their arms back and forth to simulate trees blowing in the wind*], and he saw many interesting animals, including _____ [*find volunteers to take each animal puppet, and bring them forward to hold their animals*].

The old man saw all these animals wandering around in the forest. [*Send the puppeteers out wan-*

The old man said: "Don't cry, rabbit. What's the matter?"

The rabbit was finally able to speak: "I couldn't find anything for you to eat. I feel so sad."

"That's all right," replied the old man. "The other animals brought me many things to eat."

Then the rabbit, who truly wanted to help the old man, had an idea and said: "Old man, if you are so hungry that you are starving, I have an idea. I want to save your life. You could build a big bonfire…and then you could roast me! Rabbit meat is very delicious."

The old man thought for a minute and said: "You are very kind. You mean you would be willing to give your life to help me?"

The rabbit replied: "Yes, I would — if you really needed it."

So the old man said: "You, Rabbit, are the kindest animal in the whole world. Come with me. I will carry you up in the sky, so high we will reach the moon."

And so they went together back up into the moon [*have the two climb back up on the chair and have the two puppets position themselves next to one another and cover them both with the scarf*].

Do you know that in Japan, and in many other Asian countries today, if you look at the full moon, you don't see a picture of the man in the moon, but instead you can easily see the face of a [*have the children respond: "…rabbit in the moon!"*].

3. Conclude the skit by introducing each of the puppeteers, followed by encouraged and enthusiastic applause.

Discussion Questions

1. All the animals helped the old man. Why was the rabbit the kindest?

2. What are some ways you can be like the rabbit (giving of your very self or sharing something you love a lot)? at home? at school? in your community? in the larger world?

3. What are some ways your country can be like the rabbit?

Follow-up Activities

1. *Other folktales:* Share with your children or ask them to find other folktales from different countries or peoples that also focus on sharing. Compare the messages. Discuss their implications for the children's own lives. Three excellent sources are:

- *Fifth World Tales,* Children's Book Press (1461 9th Ave., San Francisco, CA 94122), is a series of brightly illustrated storybooks for grades K–6. The stories spring from Latino, Chicano, Asian, Afro-American, and Native American communities.

- UNICEF is another source.

- *Try on My Shoe* is Camy Condon's 72-page book on multicultural puppetry with folktales from East Africa, Mexico, and Vietnam. Order from Lynne Jennings, 281 E. Millan St., Chula Vista, CA 92010.

2. *Being a "rabbit":* Have the children think of one way they could be like the rabbit, and then ask them to follow through on that action. Have them share their action and their feelings about it as a group, followed by a group celebration (in a religious setting, this celebration should include prayer/worship). In addition to, or instead of, individual "rabbit" actions, you and your children could decide on a group action.

3. *Historical and contemporary "rabbits":* Ask the children to name people they consider to be like "rabbits," either historical figures or contemporary persons, and why they consider them "rabbits." The children could also do a short report, with pictures if possible, on a famous "rabbit," i.e., someone who gave his or her life to help others. These might be posted on the "world heroes bulletin board" described in THE WORLD IN A BASKET, p. 52, perhaps renamed the "rabbit bulletin board." Two excellent resources on famous "rabbit" peacemakers are:

- Cornelia Lehn, *Peace Be with You,* Faith and Life Press, 1980. The actual stories of historical and contemporary peacemakers.

- the unit on "Today's Peacemakers" in *Educating for Peace and Justice: A Manual for Teachers,* vol. 3 (Institute for Peace and Justice).

4. *Religious reflection:* In a religious education setting, it will be important to reflect on how our faith calls us to be "rabbits." For Jews, it is the example of the Hebrew prophets, the "suffering servant" of Isaiah, and God's own steadfast love. For Christians, it is also the example of Jesus, his cross and resurrection. "Those who lose their life for my sake will find it...." "Unless the seed fall into the ground and die, it cannot bear fruit...."

Further Resources

Part I contains several skits on peacemaking and peacemakers that provide many additional activities and resources and a variety of children's books. The story of *Sadako and the Thousand Paper Cranes* (available from the Fellowship of Reconciliation, Box 271, Nyack, NY 10960) is especially appropriate, as she died trying to make a thousand paper cranes as a plea for peace as well as for her own life. See THE JAPANESE FARM WOMAN, p. 19 above, for other variations of the Sadako story.

Children's books include:

The Giving Tree, by Shel Silverstein, Harper, 1962. The story of how a tree sacrifices itself for a man, responding to his needs.

The King, the Mice and the Cheese, by Nancy Gurney, Beginner Books, 1965. This is a fine book to help young children start their understanding of sharing.

The Story of Jumping Mouse, by John Steptoe, Lothrop, Lee and Shepard Books, 1984. This Native American legend invites children to take risks in giving themselves and pursuing their dreams. A wonderful allegory!

The River That Gave Gifts, by Margo Humphrey, Children's Book Press, 1978. In this fine Afro-American story, four children in an African village make special gifts for an elder, who is going blind.

Toad Is the Uncle of Heaven, retold and illustrated by Jeanne M. Lee, Holt, Rinehart & Winston, 1985. An amusing Vietnamese folktale about how the ugly toad cooperated with other animals to save the earth from drought.

18

100 HUNGRY PEOPLE

Theme and Format

This silent dramatization graphically illustrates the reality of the maldistribution of the world's resources, using food as the specific example. It requires children to interpret the dramatization and then invites them to think of ways they can work to change this national as well as global injustice.

Directions

Note: one option is to show your children the videotape version of this dramatization, stopping before the explanation/discussion. If you show the videotape, the numbers and percentages will be different from those below. We revised these for this book to reflect actual statistics more accurately. But the main point remains in both — the vast majority of the world's population has relatively little while a select few have an enormous amount.

1. *Materials:*

- 3 card tables, preferably each covered with a different color table cloth

% of world population = cups
% of world resources = cereal

- 100 small paper cups
- 1 sign reading "100 HUNGRY PEOPLE" on one side and "75 HUNGRY PEOPLE" on the other
- 3 boxes of the same breakfast cereal, preferably "LIFE" cereal (because of its powerful symbolism)
- 1 puppet (wearing a chef's hat, if possible; a pig puppet would suggest a hint of "pigging out" and other touches of "eating like a pig")

2. *Arrangement of the materials:* The arrangement can be done ahead of time or can be part of the dramatization itself. In the second case, start with all 100 paper cups on one table, with the sign reading "100 HUNGRY PEOPLE" taped to the front (100 represents 100 percent of the people living on earth). Have the puppet transfer 25 of the cups to the second table and then 6 of these 25 to the third table. The first table with 75 cups (75 percent of the world's population) represents the hungry "Third World" (Africa, Asia, and Latin America). The second and third tables represent the "First World" (Western capitalist countries) and the "Second World" (U.S.S.R. and the Eastern European communist countries), with the third table being just the United States, with 6 cups (6 percent of the world's population). The puppet should flip over the sign on the "Third World table" so that it reads "75 HUNGRY PEOPLE."

3. The cereal represents all the basic resources of the earth, especially food. Pour the 3 boxes of LIFE cereal into the cups to reflect the maldistribution of the world's resources: roughly 75 percent of the world's population have access to only about 25 percent of the world's resources, while the United States, with only 6 percent of the world's population, consumes about 40 percent of the world's resources.

- The chef pours the first box of LIFE into the 75 cups on the "Third World table," but with a little of it also poured into the cups on the second table. Set the empty box mostly on the "Third World table."

- The chef pours the second box primarily into the cups on the second table, but with some of it going into the 6 cups on the "U.S. table." Set the empty box mostly on the second table.

- The chef pours the third box completely into the 6 cups on the "U.S. table," causing the cereal to overflow these cups and spill all over the table. Set the empty box completely on this table.

- Finally, in order to reflect even more accurately the maldistribution of resources—the realities of hunger within the U.S. and the wealth of a few in the Third World—have the puppet pour most of the cereal from at least 1 of the 6 U.S. cups and some of the cereal from 3 more U.S. cups into the remaining 2 U.S. cups; then pour the cereal from a number of the 75 Third World cups into 2 of the Third World cups so that they overflow. The skit ends.

4. Ask the children to interpret what the cups, the cereal, and the tables represent, and then guess what the puppet was doing in each step. This will probably require some clues, but as much as possible see if the children can figure out what was being dramatized.

Discussion Questions

1. On which of the tables are you and I living today?
2. Is there something wrong or unfair about this situation? If so, what?
3. What would make that situation fair?
4. Why don't some people in the United States have enough food?
5. Why don't most people in the Third World have enough food?
6. What can we do about changing the situation for the hungry in our own country?
7. What can we do about changing the situation for the hungry in the Third World?

Follow-up Activities

1. *A paper plate alternative:* Distribute a paper plate to each child and have each divide the plate into three equal sections. Draw circles for the number of persons in each section as illustrated in the dramatization. Have them show in some way how the resources are presently maldistributed— e.g., mostly tiny circles in the Third World section and only partially colored in and a few large ones fully colored in; mostly larger circles in the second section fully colored in with a few exceptions; several still larger circles in the third section fully colored, or perhaps the larger circles could be colored beyond their boundaries to illustrate having much more than they need.

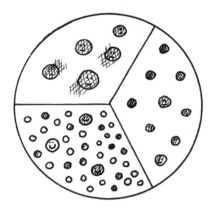

After comparing different children's representations, give them a second paper plate and ask them to design their world the way they think it should be.

2. *Some sensitizing experiences of hunger*:*

- For middle-grade students and older, have them visit a local house of hospitality (e.g., the Catholic Worker, the Salvation Army) at meal time, and if possible, assist in the preparation and serving of the meal.

- For the primary grades and up, have students, preferably with some parents, visit a local open-air farmers' market some Saturday afternoon to pick up the usable produce that has been thrown behind the stalls. (To experience what many poor people do for a meal, prepare a group meal with the produce gathered, with the children helping with the cooking.)

- For primary grades, have a "Third World Party," one in which one-third of the class gets several cookies, while two-thirds gets a part of a soda

---

*Taken from the unit on "Hunger" in *Educating for Peace and Justice: Global Dimensions,* Institute for Peace and Justice.

cracker. Students can share but they are not required to do so.

- For middle-grade students and older, have a "Third World Banquet," at which one-third of the group is served a banquet dinner while the other two-thirds are served a poverty meal. A poverty meal is the typical meal of a poor person in another part of the world or in one's own area. A little bread, rice, and water would be typical for parts of Asia. A small portion of refried beans would be typical for parts of Latin America. The well-fed one-third might choose to share but they might not.

For more details, write CROP, Box 968, Elkhart, IN 46514. A word of caution here: to actually experience any of these sensitizing experiences will raise a complex of emotions — anger, guilt, embarrassment. It is crucial to spend a long time reflecting on the experience and, as part of this reflection, to examine ways in which people can act on the issue of hunger. To guide such an experience, a teacher must be a perceptive de-briefer, because such "have/have not" experiences can be volatile.

3. *Film on world hunger:* An alternative way of putting faces on the realities of world hunger is through audio-visuals. One of the best films appropriate for 10- to 13-year-olds is *Faces of My Brothers and Sisters,* a 7-minute depiction of both hungry Third World people and ignorance about the Third World among North Americans; produced by and available from Maryknoll Films, Maryknoll, NY 10545.

4. *Some action projects:*

- UNICEF. Collecting money for UNICEF, especially at Halloween, is a traditional way for young children to respond. Showing a UNICEF film beforehand adds to the experience.

- CROP walk. Walk-a-thons, bike-a-thons, etc., are another traditional fund-raising effort. Challenge the creativity of your children to design their own _____-a-thon (e.g., read-a-thon: pledges for every book read).

- Heifer Project (HP). This forty-year effort to purchase animals and promote self-help for the hungry of the Third World has many children's possibilities. One of the many described in *Reaching Out...to Lend a Helping Hand* (fifty-seven fund-raising ideas from the HP, P.O. Box 808, Little Rock, AR 72203) is called "Love Day." Have the children make a Valentine box. Display printed pictures of all HP animals (cows, sheep, pigs, rabbits, chicks, goats). Near Valentine's Day, ask children to bring a donation as a love-gift to help buy a "living gift" for a hungry child. Children place their donations in the Valentine box and in exchange are given an HP Valentine. When the love-gifts are in, send them to HP. Christmas cards to friends can include "A Share" in an HP animal. Printed cards are available from HP.

- Political action. Writing letters (younger children can draw pictures) to political representatives for legislation to help the hungry is crucial. Local Bread for the World representatives are helpful in explaining the legislative process as well as specific pieces of legislation and the realities of world hunger for middle grades and junior high (contact the BFW national office — 802 Rhode Island Ave., N.E., Washington, DC 20018 — if you need help finding them).

Further Resources

For older children, the Institute for Food and Development Policy (1885 Mission Street, San Francisco, CA 94103) has developed a hunger curriculum that examines the causes of world hunger. A comic book version of their analysis is also available for junior high children in the July 1983 issue of *New Internationalist.*

Hunger Activities for Children is a 120-page book of classroom activities and actions especially helpful to elementary religious educators; published by Brethren House, 6301 56th Ave. N., St. Petersburg, FL 33709.

19

WHERE'S IT FROM?
THE JOURNEY OF THE POLYESTER BLOUSE

Theme and Format

People in many countries contribute to the making of products we take for granted. This skit traces the global assembly line used in making one simple blouse. It usually surprises everyone. About half of all goods produced today travel to more than one country.

Directions

1. *Materials:*

- a polyester blouse or skirt, any size, on a hanger
- a globe
- 8 pieces of construction paper or large cards numbered 1–8
- 1 hand-puppet narrator

2. Print the numbers with appropriate country on the front side of the paper or cards. Print the simple script on the back of each card.

Front Side:

1 El Salvador	2 South Carolina U.S.A.	3 Venezuela	4 Trinidad
5 New Jersey U.S.A	6 North Carolina U.S.A.	7 Haiti	8 New York U.S.A.

Sources for WHERE'S IT FROM?: Adapted with permission from a poster available from *Seeds* magazine, June 1987, 222 East Lake Drive, Decatur, GA 30030; poster cost: $2.50; originally an article by John Cavenagh in *Response: The Journal of United Methodist Women*, 1985.

Back Side:

1. *El Salvador*
Workers in a poor province of El Salvador plant and harvest for our blouse. There is a war nearby. Children and adults pick the cotton on

long hot days. Adults earn about $2 (U.S.) a day, which is less than 1 percent of the final value of our blouse. The government of El Salvador has diverted millions of pesos from health and education projects to pay for the guns and equipment used in the war.

2. *South Carolina, U.S.A.*
The ginned cotton is shipped to South Carolina in the U.S.A. by a company called Cargill. This company can bargain for a very cheap price with the Salvadoran landowner. In South Carolina, the cotton is sold to Burlington for spinning into thread. Burlington is the largest textile mill in the U.S.A.

3. *Venezuela*
   Next we need oil from Venezuela, because polyester is made from petroleum. In South America, Venezuelan workers have a dangerous job

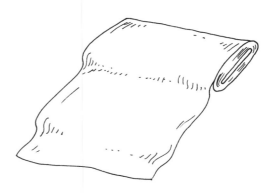

drilling and processing oil. They work under hot skies for about $6 (U.S.) a day. After they pump and refine the oil for the state company, the oil is sold to Exxon, a giant multinational corporation. Exxon controls the most profitable part of the oil business, the processing, marketing, and final distribution of the oil.

4. *Trinidad*
   Exxon carries the oil by ship to the islands of Trinidad and Tobago. Here the oil is processed again into many petrochemicals. The work is difficult, dangerous, and unhealthy because many of the chemicals are poisonous.

5. *New Jersey, U.S.A.*
   The chemicals are put on another ship and sent to New Jersey. They go to a big DuPont factory where they speed through huge machines and come out as miles and miles of continuous string called filament. This is the polyester part of the thread.

6. *North Carolina, U.S.A.*
   The polyester thread is taken to another Burlington textile mill. The workers' salaries are very low. Here high-powered looms combine the cotton thread from South Carolina with the

polyester chemical thread. Then the combined threads are woven into long sheets of fabrics ready to be cut into our blouse pattern.

A big retail company, like Sears, comes to buy the woven cloth. Eventually this company will sell the blouse.

7. *Haiti*
   The polyester and cotton cloth is put onto another ship. It's carried to Haiti. Small Haitian-owned-and-run businesses pay women workers about $3 (U.S.) a day to make the blouse. The

Haitian women bend over the sewing machines for long hours stitching seams. They have no labor union. They will be fired or punished if they talk about changing their working conditions.

8. *New York, U.S.A.*
The finished blouses leave the "Third World" for the last time. They are put on *another* ship and sent back to U.S.A. to New York. In New York, the blouses are packaged and sealed in plastic and finally sent to mail order buyers around the U.S.A.

We find the blouses on display at our local department store, and we buy one.

3. *Puppet Narrator:* The puppet narrator acts as an MC for the journey of the blouse. The eight country cards are distributed throughout the audience to older children or adults. One child is invited to hold the blouse on its hanger and carry it throughout the audience to each numbered country. The puppet narrator begins by saying:

"Ladies and gentlemen. Welcome to the world of the global assembly line. How many of you in our audience are wearing something made out of polyester and cotton cloth? Maybe you have a white handkerchief of this material. Today we will look at its amazing journey. First we go to no. 1, El Salvador."

The puppet narrator improvises a simple transition from number to number, country to country.

4. To visualize the journey more fully, do one of the following: Have a child hold the globe and point to each country and state as it is featured. Or with pins and yarn on a world map or on a cloth globe,

make lines between the eight locations on the journey.

Discussion Questions

1. Why are so many states and countries involved in making just one simple item like a blouse?

2. What would happen if people made their own clothes, as Gandhi tried to do in India?

3. What happens in all the other states and countries if change takes place in one of them (e.g., a strike by workers in South Carolina or in El Salvador for fairer wages, or a big drop in the price of oil for Venezuela, or a drought ruining half the cotton crop in El Salvador)?

4. What practices do you think are unfair in any of the steps in the process?

5. What can we do to make any of these unfair practices less unfair?

Follow-up Activities

1. *Hershey Bar:* For groups of younger children, do a similar but simpler activity focusing on the ingredients in a Hershey Bar. Ingredients and sources for the Hershey Bar include:

- chocolate/cocoa from Ghana
- almonds from Brazil
- sugar from the Dominican Republic
- milk from Pennsylvania dairy farms
- corn syrup from Iowa corn fields
- paper wrappers from Canadian lumber mills
- stores selling Hershey Bars in many cities, states, countries

One benefit of using the Hershey Bar is the wealth of posters, booklets, and other interesting educational resources available from the Hershey Corporation itself in Hershey, PA 17033.

2. *"Discovering Global Connections"*: See pp. 52 above.

3. *"The Banana Connections"*: Much of the food we eat comes from other parts of the world. Before it gets to our tables, its production often involves exploitation. Bananas, for instance, come from Central American countries and the Philippines, where those who pick the bananas are grossly underpaid. In the Philippines, these workers generally receive about $1.50 a day. In many cases, the workers were formerly self-sufficient rice farmers who lost their land to banana corporations like Del Monte. Instead of eating the rice they once grew for themselves, these farmers have to buy it. How far will their $1.50/day go in feeding their family? We can connect ourselves with these workers, become more conscious of the benefits we enjoy at their expense, and respond to their exploitation through a series of steps:

- Whenever we buy bananas, charge ourselves an extra amount, say 20 percent, to represent the additional amount we would pay if the corporation involved paid the banana pickers a just wage. Some families do this by charging themselves a penny each time a family member eats a banana so that the connection is made more often and by each family member (not just the shopper).

- Place the money set aside in a container decorated, for instance, with a map of the Philippines, a banana label or sticker, and a picture of an agricultural worker.

- Send the collection periodically to a group working with those who are being exploited in the process. Possibilities for Philippines banana workers include Jubilee Crafts (see below) and various church groups like the Maryknoll Sisters, Maryknoll, NY 10545. Designate the money for the Philippines and ask the group to get it as close to the workers as possible — those from whom the money was withheld, as it were, in the first place.

4. *"Third World" gifts:* Another action possibility is to buy the handicrafts of Third World people at gift-giving times and to organize an alternative gift-giving bazaar for the school (or church) at Hanukkah/Christmas. The *Alternative Celebrations*

Catalog (from Alternatives, Box 429, Ellenwood, GA 30049), itself an ideal gift, contains the names, addresses, and descriptions of a variety of outlets for Third World handicrafts like Jubilee Crafts (Box 12236, Philadelphia, PA 19144), which makes available the handicrafts of widows in Bangladesh and of other craft cooperatives in Haiti, the Philippines, Central America, and elsewhere.

5. *"Pairing" with a Third World group:* "Pairing" provides concreteness to the general term "Third World." It puts students in touch with people working for social change and probably paying a price for their commitment, which should help inspire the students. It offers a channel for Third World concerns to enter our communities and offers the possibility of long-term action and relationship. Possibilities include:

- *Schools.* MADRE (853 Broadway, New York, NY 10001; tel.: 212-674-7763) has paired more than twenty-five U.S. day-care centers and preschools with Nicaraguan counterparts. These generally involve exchanges of the children's pictures and drawings, educational aid collections and shipments, and parent education programs. MADRE is also promoting pairings between medical personnel, teachers, and women in general.

- *Educational Aid.* As part of its Quest for Peace effort, the Quixote Center continues to encourage schools, classes, and individual children to "clean out their desks" for Nicaragua, not only at the end of the year but anytime. While all kinds of educational supplies are needed, most helpful are pencils and pens, paper of all kinds, chalk and chalk boards. Flyers are available from Quixote Center, P.O. Box 5206, Hyattsville, MD 20782; tel.: 301-699-0042.

- *Families/Children.* The "Godparent Project" of the Ecumenical Refugee Council (2510 N. Frederich, Milwaukee, WI 53211; tel.: 414-332-5461) is currently sponsoring more than 250 orphans in six orphanages throughout Nicaragua. North American families contributing a minimum of $10 a month are paired with a specific child they are supporting financially and whose picture they receive.

6. *The earth as a single system or interconnected whole:* It is important at some point to take our awareness beyond our connectedness as a single human family to the interconnectedness of the earth itself. On the more abstract level, ask the children to name some of the subsystems that make up the world—water, air, land, food, people. Have them name ways these subsystems work together, then some problems facing each subsystem. Brainstorm together on what happens to the other subsystems when something bad happens to one of the subsystems (e.g., flood, drought, polluted air, leaks of nuclear waste materials).

To affirm the unity and sacredness of the earth, do the following:

- *World Pledge:* After children have discussed the World Pledge, help them to brainstorm and determine concrete ways of daily living the pledge. Younger children can color and display their pledges as well as their concrete actions.

> I pledge allegiance to the world
> to cherish every living thing,
> to care for earth and sea and air
> with peace and freedom everywhere!

- *Hug-a-Planet:* Cloth earth balls make a wonderful huggable home or classroom resource. Available from XTC Products, 247 Rockingtone Ave., Larchmont, NY 10538, in 3 sizes (6", 12", and 24" diameters), these, and inflatable plastic globe counterparts, can serve as maps, as balls to toss carefully while singing, "We've Got the Whole World in Our Hands," and as a visual reminder of our interconnectedness.

- *"Earth Walks" and other earth awareness activities:* Simple sensory explorations of our environment (home, school, church lot, neighborhood, parks, forests) can open up our hearts as well as our minds and provide a wealth of activities for nurturing reverence for the earth and fostering a thankful religious spirit and artistic expression. An excellent resource for parents and teachers is *Sharing Nature with Children: A Parents and Teachers Nature-Awareness Guidebook,* by Joseph Cornell, Dawn Publications (14618 Tyler Foot Road, Nevada City, CA 95959), 1979.

- *Chief Seattle and the Earth:* The 1854 letter of Chief Seattle to the president of the United States in response to a request to buy the lands of the Suquamish people in the Seattle, Washington, area, is a beautiful expression of our interconnectedness with the earth and how we are to love and care for the earth as our "mother," as the following excerpts indicate:

> Teach your children what we have taught our children, that the earth is our mother. Whatever befalls the earth, befalls the children of the earth. If we spit upon the ground, we spit upon ourselves. This we know. The earth does not belong to us; we belong to the earth....
>
> One thing we know, which the white man may one day discover—our God is the same God. You may think now that you own God as you wish to own our land; but you cannot. Our God is the God of all people, and God's compassion is equal for all. This earth is precious to God, and to harm the earth is to heap contempt on its Creator....
>
> So love it as we have loved it. Care for it as we have cared for it. And with all your strength, with all your mind, with all your heart, preserve it for your children, and love it, as God loves us all.

Further Resources

For adults, especially teachers, *Educating for Peace and Justice: Global Dimensions* has excellent units on "Global Interdependence," with case studies on the Philippines, Nicaragua, and El Salvador for older students, and a special section on "interdependence" for elementary students.

20

RECOMMENDED BOOKS

Young Children (Preschool to grade 3)

Africans and Black Americans

Count on Your Fingers African Style, by Claudia Zaslavsky, illustrated by Jerry Pinkney, Thomas Y. Crowell, 1980.

The River That Gave Gifts, written and illustrated by Margo Humphrey, Children's Book Press (1461 Ninth Avenue, San Francisco, CA 94122), 1978.

My Mama Needs Me, by Mildred Pitts Walter, illustrated by Pat Cummings, Lothrop, Lee & Shepard, 1983.

Jambo Means Hello, Swahili Alphabet Book, by Muriel Feelings, illustrated by Tom Feelings, Dial Press, 1974.

Moja Means One, Swahili Counting Book, by Muriel Feelings, illustrated by Tom Feelings, Dial Press, 1971.

I Can Do It By Myself, by Leslie Jones Little and Eloise Greenfield, illustrated by Carole Byard, Thomas Y. Crowell, 1978.

Brown Spices ABC Book: A Great Coloring Book for Boys and Girls, by Annie and Julee, Brown Spices Publishing Co. (P.O. Box 29397, Washington, D.C. 20017-0397), 1984. This is an imaginative coloring book that celebrates the unity of Black families.

Grandmama's Joy, by Eloise Greenfield, illustrated by Carole Byard, Collins Publishers, 1980.

Honey, I Love and Other Poems, by Eloise Greenfield, illustrated by Diane and Leo Dillon, Thomas Y. Crowell, 1978.

My Friend Jacob, by Lucille Clifton, illustrated by Thomas De Grazia, Harper and Row, 1980.

Rosa Parks, by Eloise Greenfield, Thomas Y. Crowell, 1973. This book sensitively depicts the indignities endured by Black people in our recent past and the quiet courage of "the Mother of the Civil Rights Movement" in bravely claiming her rights.

African Dream, by Eloise Greenfield, illustrated by Carole Byard, John Day Co., 1977. The soft, flowing illustrations in this book are very fitting for a story about a Black child's dream trip to Africa of long ago. There is a good linkage between Black Americans and their African roots.

The Quilt, written and illustrated by Ann Jonas, Greenwillow Books, 1984.

Star Boy, written and illustrated by Paul Goble, Bradbury Press, 1983.

Native Americans

Moonsong Lullaby, photographs by Marcia Keegan, Lothrop, Lee & Shepard, 1981.

The Goat in the Rug, by Charles Blood and Marcia Link, illustrated by Nancy Winslow Parker, Parents Magazine Press, 1976.

Arrow to the Sun: A Pueblo Indian Myth, by Gerald McDermott, Viking Press, 1975.

Annie and the Old One, by Miska Miles, illustrated by Peter Parnall, Little, Brown, 1971. Through her grandmother, a respected Navajo elder, Annie learns a valuable lesson about growth and change and death.

Hispanics

My Mother the Mail Carrier? Mi Mamá la Cartera?, by Inez Maury, illustrated by Lady McGrady, Feminist Press, 1976.

Yagua Days, by Cruz Martel, illustrated by Jerry Pincknery, Dial Press, 1976. Puerto Rican.

I Am Here: Yo Estoy Aquí, by Rose Blue, illustrated by Moneta Barnett, Franklin Watts, 1971.

Idalia's Project ABC: An Urban Alphabet Book in English and Spanish, written and illustrated by Idalia Rosario, Holt, Rinehart and Winston, 1981.

Asians and Asian Americans

First Snow, by Helen Coutant, illustrated by Vo-Dinh, Knopf, 1974.

Umbrella, by Taro Yashima, Penguin Books, 1977.

Aekyung's Dream, by Min Peak, Children's Book Press, 1978. This beautifully illustrated bilingual book tells the story of a young Korean girl, newly arrived in the United States, who finds strength in a dream about Korean history.

Crow Boy, by Taro Yashima, Penguin Books, 1976. This sensitive story, which takes place in a Japanese setting, is about a universal experience of childhood, the struggle to gain acceptance. The book includes some highlights of Japanese culture.

Toad Is the Uncle of Heaven, retold and illustrated by Jeanne M. Lee, Holt, Rinehart and Winston, 1985. An amusing Vietnamese folktale about how an ugly toad cooperated with other animals to save the earth from drought.

Multicultural

All About Me, by Jackie Weisman, photographs by David L. Giveans, Acropolis Books, Ltd. (available from D.L. Giveans, 187 Caselli Ave., San Francisco, CA 94114), 1981, 45 rpm record for book also available.

Why Am I Different? by Norma Simon, illustrated by Dora Leder, Albert Whitman & Co., 1976.

Living in Two Worlds, by Maxine Rosenberg, photographs by George Ancona, Lothrop, Lee & Shepard, 1986.

Middle Grades

Africans and Black Americans

Black Child, by Joyce Carol Thomas, illustrated by Tom Feelings, Zamani Productions (31 W. 31st St., New York, NY 10001), 1981.

Alesia, by Eloise Greenfield and Alesia Revis, illustrated by George Ford with photos by Sandra Turner Bond, Philomel Books (Putnam), 1981.

Song of the Trees, by Mildred D. Taylor, illustrated by Judy Pinkney, Dial, 1975.

Paul Robeson, by Eloise Greenfield, illustrated by George Ford, Thomas Y. Crowell, 1975

Daydreamers, by Tom Feelings and Eloise Greenfield, Dial, 1981.

Fannie Lou Harner, by June Jordan, Thomas Y. Crowell, 1975.

Apples on a Stick: The Folklore of Black Children, collected and edited by Barbara Michels and Bettye White, illustrated by Jerry Pinkney, Coward McCann, 1983.

Paris, Pee Wee, and Big Dog, by Rosa Guy, illustrated by Caroline Binch, Delacorte, 1985.

Southern Africa, by Harry Stein, Franklin Watts, 1975.

Native Americans

Groundhog's Horse, by Joyce Rockwood, Holt, Rinehart and Winston, 1978.

An Eskimo's Birthday, by Tom D. Robinson, illustrated by Glo Coalson, Dodd, Mead.

Tonweya and the Eagles and Other Lakota Indian Tales, by Rosebud Yellow Robe, illustrated by Jerry Pinkney, Dial Press, 1979.

Buffalo Woman, written and illustrated by Paul Goble, Bradbury, 1984.

The Tipi: A Center of Native American Life, by Charlotte and David Yoe, Knopf, 1984.

Hispanics

Maria Teresa, by Mary Atkinson, illustrated by Christine Engla Eber, Lollipop Power, 1979.

Roberto Clemente, by Kenneth Rudeen, illustrated by Frank Mullins, Thomas Y. Crowell, 1974.

Piñata and Paper Flowers/Piñata y Flores de Papel: Holidays of the Americas, English and Spanish by Lila Perl, translated by Alma Flor Ada, illustrated by Victoria de Larrea, Clarion Books, 1983.

Felita, by Nicholasa Mohr, illustrated by Ray Cruz, Dial, 1979.

Asians and Asian Americans

The Crane Wife, retold by Sumiko Yagawa, translation from the Japanese by Katherine Patersen, illustrated by Suekichi Akaba, Morrow Junior Books, 1981.

Sing to the Dawn, by Minfong Ho, illustrated by Kwoncjon Ho, Lothrop, Lee & Shepard, 1975.

Sadako and the Thousand Paper Cranes, by Eleanor Coerr, Dell Yearling Book, 1977.

The Chinese Word for Horse and Other Stories, by John Lewis, illustrated by Peter Rigby, Schocken Books, 1980.

An Album of Chinese Americans, by Betty Lee Sung, Franklin Watts, 1977.

The Happiest Ending, by Yoshiko Uchida, Atheneum, 1985.

Jewish Americans

A Gift for Mama, by Esther Hautzig, illustrated by Donna Diamond, Viking, 1981.

Toba, by Michael Marl, illustrated by Neil Waldman, Bradbury Press, 1984.

Night Journey, by Kathryn Lasky, illustrated by Trina Schart Hyman, Puffin, 1986.

Older Students (Grades 7 and up)

Africans and Black Americans

Du Bois: A Pictorial Biography, by Shirley Graham Du Bois, Johnson Publishing Co., 1979.

Talk About a Family, by Eloise Greenfield, illustrated by James Calvin, J.B. Lippincott Co., 1978.

Roll of Thunder, Hear My Cry, by Mildred Taylor, illustrated by Jerry Pinkney, Dial, 1976.

Black Child, by Peter Magubane, Knopf, 1982.

Shaka, King of the Zulus, by Daniel Cohen, Doubleday, 1973.

The Magical Adventures of Pretty Pearl, by Virginia Hamilton, Harper & Row, 1983.

Martin Luther King, Jr.: A Man to Remember, by Patricia McKissack, Children's Press, 1984.

Motown and Didi, by Walter Dean Myers, Viking, 1984.

Martin Luther King, The Man Who Climbed the Mountain, by Gary Paulsen and Dan Theis, Raintree (distributed by Children's Press), 1976.

Junius Over Far, by Virginia Hamilton, Harper & Row, 1985.

Native Americans

This Song Remembers: Self-Portraits of Native Americans in the Arts, ed. Jane B. Katz, Houghton Mifflin, 1980.

Let Me Be a Free Man, by Jane B. Katz, Lerner, 1975.

Native Americans: 500 Years After, photographs by Joseph C. Farber, text by Michael Dorris, Thomas Y. Crowell, 1975.

The Ways of My Grandmothers, by Beverly Hungry Wolf, illustrated with photos, Morrow, 1980.

Barefoot a Thousand Miles, by Patsey Gray, Walker, 1984.

American Indian Myths and Legends, selected and edited by Richard Erdoes and Alfonso Ortiz, illustrated by Richard Erdoes, Pantheon, 1984. An anthology of 166 legends and myths from many Native American peoples, organized around themes. Gives a clear message that Native Americans are still living today with a valuable culture.

Hispanics

The Hispanic Americans, by Milton Melzer, illustrated by Catherine Noren and Morrie Camhi, Thomas Y. Crowell, 1982.

Mexican American Movement and Leaders, by Carlos Larralde, Hwong Publishing Co.

Alicia Alonso: The Story of a Ballerina, by Beatrice Siegal, Frederick Warne, 1979. The biography of the famous Cuban ballerina gives the reader glimpses of Cuban history as well as a personal story of struggle against sexism, the physical disability of blindness, and the hardship of learning to survive in a new culture.

Stories from El Barrio, 12/6, by Piri Thomas, Knopf, 1978.

Revolutionary Cuba, by Terence Cannon, Thomas Y. Crowell, 1981.

Asians and Asian Americans

Journey Home, by Yoshiko Uchida, Atheneum Publishers, 1978.

Dragonwings, by Lawrence Yep, Harper & Row, 1975. Through the story of Moon Shadow and his relation with his father, this book gives an indepth look at the rich traditions of the Chinese community in a hostile world.

Child of the Owl, by Lawrence Yep, Harper & Row, 1977. A beautifully sensitive story of a Chinese-American girl, Casey, who begins to mature as she grows in her understanding of Chinatown and what it means to be Chinese.

The Chinese Americans, by Milton Meltzer, Thomas Y. Crowell, 1980.

The Serpent's Children, by Lawrence Yep, Harper & Row, 1984. Will help readers, young and old, counter stereotypic views of the Chinese. Characters are real people. Both Cassia and Foxfire are positive, non-sexist heroes.

Linking Our Lives: Chinese American Women of Los Angeles, Chinese Historical Society (Book Dept., 4205 S. Lasalle Ave., Los Angeles, CA 90062), 1984.

Jewish Americans

The Jewish Americans: A History in Their Own Words, 1650–1950, by Milton Meltzer, Thomas Y. Crowell, 1982.

In Kindling Flame: The Story of Hannah Senesh, 1921–1944, by Linda Atkinson, Lothrop, Lee & Shepard, 1985. An inspiring story of a young woman's heroism and a welcome addition to the literature of Jewish resistance.

Multicultural

Morning Glory Afternoon, by Irene Bennet Brown, Atheneum, 1981.

The Piano Makers, by David Anderson, Pantheon Books, 1982.

Northern Fried Chicken, by Roni Schotter, Philomel Books (Putnam), 1983.

It's Aardvark-Eat-Turtle World, by Paula Danziger, Delacorte, 1985.

On Fire, by Ouida Sebestyen, Atlantic Monthly Press, 1985.

Author Camy Condon, with part of her collection of multicultural puppets, demonstrates the "World in a Basket" (see p. 52). In the background, the tables are set for "100 Hungry People" (see p. 65).

Camy Condon fosters global awareness and appreciation of other cultures through intergenerational and participatory puppet shows.

Part III

AGING AWARENESS

21

TWENTY QUESTIONS:
AN AGING INFORMATION QUIZ FOR EVERYBODY

Theme and Format

This is an intergenerational community quiz about the aging population of the United States. Two paper bag puppets involve the audience in guessing True or False by raising one or two fingers of their hand after each question is asked. There are no winners or losers, but everyone becomes better informed after finding out if the guesses are correct or not.

Directions

1. *Materials:*

- 2 paper bag puppets (or hand puppets)
- a grandmother and a grandchild (girl or boy)
- 2 cloth-covered chairs for each to hide behind (optional)
- a copy of the script and twenty questions for each puppeteer

2. *Opening Dialogue:*

GRANDMOTHER: Well, well, well. Look at all the folks out there. How nice everyone came to our Aging Quiz today. Do you think they're ready?

GRANDCHILD: Sure, Grandma. They look pretty smart. But I bet we can catch them on a few of these. It's a hot topic, Grandma, and *you* are an expert.

GRANDMOTHER: Thanks, dear. Let's tell them about guessing with their fingers. Since it's a true or false quiz, they can raise a hand showing two fingers if they think the answer is True and one finger if they think it's False. When we're finished, we'll all be experts.

GRANDCHILD: Ahem, Ahem...Ladies and Gentlemen. Welcome to Aging America. Let's see how much you know. [*Stage whisper*] Okay, Grandma, you start.

[*Grandma and grandchild alternate asking and answering the twenty questions.*]

1. Children are the fastest growing part of the U.S. population, True or False?

   GRANDMA [*Chuckles*]: TRUE and FALSE   They are the fastest growing individuals, because they get bigger every day... but senior citizens, over the age of *85,* are the fastest growing segment of the total population.   Yep, 85-year-olds and older!

2. Two hundred years ago, at the time of U.S. Independence, the average life span was 40 years, True or False?

   FALSE   It was only 30 years.   Many babies died at birth and adults did not have the benefit of immunizations to prevent major illnesses.

3. In 1900 there were 3 million American senior citizens over age 65, True or False?

   TRUE   They were 4 percent of the population.

4. In 1986 there were 29 million senior citizens in our country, True or False?

   TRUE   They were 12 percent of the population.

5. Imagine the year 2030... there will be 50 million senior citizens, True or False?

   FALSE   There will be *more*...65 million seniors, and they will be 21 percent of the population.

6. When we all get old we will probably have to live in a nursing home.

   FALSE   Only 5 percent of the older people in our communities live in nursing homes.   Most people will continue to live in their own homes or with family members.

7. Since men are pretty strong, there are more of them than women in the over-65 age group, True or False?

   FALSE   There are more older women... about 140 women for every 100 men.

8. A baby born today in our town will live (an average of) 74.5 years, True or False?

   TRUE   Women live longer, but the average is 74.5 years.

9. How many folks know someone who is a hundred years old or older? [*Looks around.*] There are about 8,000 people in the U.S. now who are a hundred years old or older, True or False?

   FALSE   There are more.   There are approximately 40,000 100-year-olds now (1987).

10. As everybody gets older all five senses (taste, touch, sight, hearing, and smell) decline, True or False?
    TRUE

11. True or False, as humans our major body organs, heart, lungs, liver, brain, were programmed to live to be 110 years old.

    TRUE   ...if disease free.

12. Sometimes people are prejudiced against older people, True or False?

    TRUE   It's called "Ageism" and a definition is: "a collection of blind prejudices and erroneous beliefs and attitudes concerning a mythical, stereotyped older person."   Can you think of any examples?

13. Teenagers can learn a foreign language faster than older people, True or False?

    FALSE   Some teens and some elders are good at learning foreign languages and some are not good.   The only age group with a distinct advantage are children up to about age 14.   Until puberty children are the most capable learners of language systems.

14. False teeth and old age go together.   We'll probably all have false teeth by the end of our lives if we live to a "ripe old age."   True or False?

    FALSE   Only about fifty percent of our elderly population needs to wear false teeth.   If good dental care is given and gum disease prevented, we all can keep chewing with our own teeth our whole life long.

15. Many older people suffer from depression, True or False?

    TRUE   Depression is the most common psychological problem of senior citizens.

16. There were 250,000 broken hips in the U.S.A. in 1986, and many of these accidents were preventable, True or False?

    TRUE   Hospital admissions and limited lifestyles could be avoided if we all work to understand how to prevent falls and resulting broken hips. Middle-age diet, safety checks in homes, and information on women and bone disease can all aid in prevention.

17. Senior citizens get stuck in their ways and have trouble adjusting to change, True or False?

    FALSE   They can and do adjust to many drastic changes: losing a spouse, moving, the death of close friends, changes in lifestyle and economic status.

18. Memory loss and confusion are just an ordinary part of growing old, True or False?

    FALSE   Many forms of confusion and memory loss can be treated, although brain diseases like Alzheimer's cannot. A frequent problem is the effects of medications on older people.

19. Older people need more light than children, True or False?

    TRUE   Lens changes sometimes cause sensitivity to glare and difficulty in distinguishing colors. People in their late fifties need 100 percent more light than 20-year-olds. An 80-year-old needs 3.5 times as much light as a 20-year-old.

20. When kids who are 18 years old today turn 65 and retire, one out of every five Americans will be senior citizens. The whole country will look like Florida's population now. True or False?

    TRUE   We will see older people everywhere. One person out of five will be a senior citizen, and there will be three times as many 85-year-olds, about 8.6 million.

3. *Closing Dialogue:*

GRANDMA: They did a good job with their guessing.

GRANDCHILD: And now we're a lot smarter about our own futures, Grandma. You know, everybody's getting older!

GRANDMA: That's right, dear. Everybody's aging. And our whole country is, too. We are living longer as senior citizens, and everything in our society will be affected by our bigger numbers. Watch out! Here we come!

GRANDCHILD: Hey, don't you mean ME? Watch out! Here WE come!

Follow-up Activities, Further Resources

See CELEBRITIES below, p. 86.

22

PORTABLE PEOPLE

Theme and Format

Profiles of outstanding senior citizens in our own communities or national or global heroes can be carried into our everyday programs by introducing them as "Portable People."

Pastel portraits, large photographs from magazines or newspapers, or simple sketches are turned into these portable guests. Two- or three-paragraph descriptions in the form of short biographies can be placed on the back of the pictures and read to the group as each celebrity is introduced.

Directions

1. Select the biographies of six interesting senior citizens who have done something extraordinary in their lives after the age of 65. They can be community people, still living and known to the group, or they can be national or international figures.

2. Find a picture of each, or a talented artist in your midst, and prepare a life-size portrait. A large magazine or newspaper photograph will also work. Put the picture on cardboard backing and tape on a flat stick to hold it up.

3. Type out the brief biographical data and tape the paper to the back of the portrait.

4. For repeated use spray both sides of the portrait with clear lacquer spray or laminate it.

5. Present the program to your group. People from the audience can be invited to assist on the spur of the moment, or six people can be prepared ahead of time to introduce their special Portable People.

6. (Optional) Older students can have their characters be part of a panel discussion about typical stereotypes people have of older persons and their accomplishments. An adult can moderate the panel, asking questions of the student panelists.

Examples of outstanding senior citizen candidates for "Portable People" are:

Grandma Moses   Frederick Douglass
Claude Pepper   Benjamin Franklin
Dorothy Day   Charles Smith
Golda Meir   Gandhi
Ruth Youngdall Nelson   Pablo Picasso
Mrs. Louis Dingwall   W. E. B. Du Bois
                 Maggie Kuhn

Samples of Short Biographies
(*Collected by Grade 3 students*)
"Let me introduce you to . . . "

GRANDMA ANNA MARY MOSES

Anna Mary Moses was best known as Grandma Moses. She was a famous painter who began her artistic career at the age of 78.

When she was young she enjoyed needlework. For many years she embroidered on canvas. But, at the age of 78 her fingers became too stiff to sew. That's when she began to paint in oils. Her brightly colored pictures of America are shown all over the world.

When Grandma Moses was 100 years old, she painted the pictures for a new book of the story " 'Twas the Night Before Christmas."

She died in 1961 at the age of 101.

MRS. LOUIS DINGWALL

Mrs. Louis Dingwall was an English grandmother and a trainer of racehorses. When she was 79 years old she applied for a license to ride in women's races.

Mrs. Dingwall rode in many races. She loved her horses. When she was 82 years old, two of her horses won on the first day of the 1975–1976 English National Hunt season. Two of her horses won the first and second races, and another was a runner-up in the third race.

CHARLES SMITH

This is Charlie Smith. He ran a small store in Florida until he was 133 years old.

In 1955, when he was 113, Charlie was still working on a citrus farm. But he was asked to retire. At the age of 113, people thought he was too old to be climbing trees.

In 1972 Charles Smith was officially recognized as the oldest person in the U.S.A. His son was 80 years old.

Charlie lived alone in the back of his store until he was 132. Then he moved into a retirement home and died a year later.

CLAUDE PEPPER

Claude Pepper is called "the Champion of the Elderly." He wears trifocals and a heart pacemaker, but at age 86 he keeps getting better and more powerful.

He was a Congressman from Miami for 20 years, and has been a U.S. Senator from Florida for 14 years. He has been a lawyer and a lifetime Democratic politician who fought for Social Security and Medicare. Claude says, "I may retire in the year 2000, but I reserve the right to change my mind."

Follow-up Activities, Further Resources

See CELEBRITIES below, p. 86.

23

PICTURE ME:
PASSING ON OUR HERITAGE

Theme and Format

Sharing life stories, faith journeys, or special feelings is the idea of this activity. One person is invited to be "pictured" briefly while telling about a life experience or something special from his or her family heritage. An empty picture frame is the object used to call attention to the message. The subject for sharing can be any number of intergenerationally interesting themes. The picture frame is passed around and each speaker uses it to frame his or her face and focus on the shared memories or bits of advice and wisdom.

Directions

In a small group, everyone can take a turn being "pictured" in the open frame. In a large group, four to eight speakers can be invited ahead of time to think about what they would like to say through the picture frame. Their messages can be the "program" or the "entertainment" for the meeting.

Any simple, used picture frame, without a picture inside, is appropriate. A simple 8" x 10" wooden frame is fine, or a lightweight, more elaborate picture frame propped up on a speaker's platform or podium can also be used.

1. *Topics for senior citizens:*

- Fond Holiday Memories
- My Favorite Proverbs
- A Bit of Wisdom
- My Journey Through Faith
- I Remember War Times
- I Remember the Depression
- How I Learned to Love
- My First Love
- A Special Cultural Tradition
- My Childhood Games and Toys

2. *Topics for children:*

- Why I Love My Grandmother (or Grandfather or a Senior Friend)
- My Visit to Older Friends in a Nursing Home
- "When I'm Old I Want to Be..."

3. *Action:* Pass the picture frame from person to person and have each speak for one to five minutes about the topic. Applause is encouraged after each speaker.

Follow-up Activities, Further Resources

See CELEBRITIES below, p. 86.

24

CELEBRITIES:
A PROGRAM OF CELEBRATION
FOR PEOPLE OVER SEVENTY-FIVE

Theme and Format

In this activity we celebrate the long lives of "ordinary" older people in our midst by inviting them to become instant "celebrities." We honor them as special and wise friends and family members.

Directions

Three to five special "celebrities" are invited to participate. In addition to the guests, the following materials are needed:

- A celebrity chair (large, comfortable, and decorated)

- A fake microphone (for humor and comfort); a large wood spoon is fine

- A few lead questions elicited from the group

Welcome the guests and introduce them informally to everyone. One at a time escort them to the special chair and tell them that the moment they sit down they will become an instant celebrity. (The chair is magic.)

The wooden-spoon microphone is the key to the interactive fun. This pretend mike is passed around among the audience members and each one takes a turn standing up and interviewing the celebrity. The first sentence for each should be a compliment or special thank you, and then a specific question should be asked.

If the celebrity is talkative and comfortable with the group, the opening five minutes can be the celebrity's own comments. However, the power of

the conversation comes from the questions everyone else comes up with.

SAMPLE COMPLIMENTS

- Thanks a lot for coming today...
- It's really nice to have you here...
- We're so glad you could come...
- You look terrific...
- Your kind voice reminds me of...
- I like your cheerful face...
- That's a pretty ring...

SAMPLE QUESTIONS ABOUT...

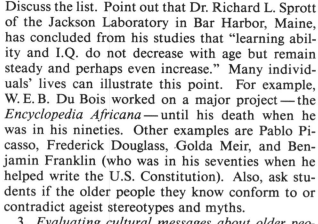

- Work
- Place of birth
- Childhood memories
- Something funny
- Something embarrassing
- Getting married
- Travels
- Holidays
- Family and children
- Hobbies or collections
- School memories
- Money seventy years ago
- Liked and disliked foods
- What your parents scolded you for
- A favorite gift given or received

Follow-up Activities

1. *Stereotypes of children:* One way to interest children in examining stereotypes about older people is to begin with stereotypes about themselves. Ask them to name all the stereotypes they can about young people. You may need to begin with a definition of stereotype. Simplify the following definition for younger students: "A stereotype can be defined as an untruth or oversimplification about the traits and actions of an entire group of people. A stereotype is applied to each member of a group, without regard to each person's individual traits."

2. *Stereotypes of older persons:* Ask students to name some stereotypes about older persons and to recall any sayings, jokes, or clichés that pertain to older people. Some possibilities are:

- "There's no fool like an old fool." (Assumes fallibility of older people and faults them for making errors, thus negating their individuality.)
- "You can't teach an old dog new tricks." (Falsely denies that old people, like the young, learn and adjust in their own individual ways.)
- "Old codger." (Is there ever a young codger?)
- "Old maid." (The term is sexist as well as ageist.)
- "Old and crotchety." (Is "crotchety" ever used without "old"?)

Discuss the list. Point out that Dr. Richard L. Sprott of the Jackson Laboratory in Bar Harbor, Maine, has concluded from his studies that "learning ability and I.Q. do not decrease with age but remain steady and perhaps even increase." Many individuals' lives can illustrate this point. For example, W. E. B. Du Bois worked on a major project — the *Encyclopedia Africana* — until his death when he was in his nineties. Other examples are Pablo Picasso, Frederick Douglass, Golda Meir, and Benjamin Franklin (who was in his seventies when he helped write the U.S. Constitution). Also, ask students if the older people they know conform to or contradict ageist stereotypes and myths.

3. *Evaluating cultural messages about older people:* Older people are often stereotyped on TV as well as in children's literature. It is important to develop children's skills in evaluating these messages. Using the following criteria and questions, have children monitor TV shows for several days and report their findings to the class; or have them each read one or two children's books and do the same.

- Some stereotypes to consider:
  - *Appearance:* face always blank and expressionless; body always bent over and infirm.
  - *Clothing:* men's is usually baggy and unpressed; women's frumpy and ill-fitting.
  - *Speech:* halting and high-pitched.
  - *Personality:* stubborn, frigid, forgetful.

- Some questions and ideas to consider:
  - Are there older people in the story or show at all?
  - If there are, are they interesting people?
  - How are they portrayed, as active, inventive, and quick-thinking, or mainly in supportive roles, or as intruders or meddlers in the relationships of others?
  - Are older people always presented as having physical disabilities?
  - Are they patronized and treated as children?
  - In comparison to others, are older people depicted as less capable? Do they have less to contribute? Are their ideas usually old-fashioned? Is the "rocking chair" image predominant?
  - Create an alternative TV show or commercial. Students acting as the famous older

persons identified in this skit could create a drama or comedy TV show or TV commercial that counteracts or makes fun of the typical stereotypes of older people.

4. *Experiencing older persons as resources:*

- Invite older people to the class to teach a skill, tell a story, or explain an element of the history of the community.

- When visiting older people, it might be best to direct children toward organizations of active, politically aware older people — the Gray Panthers, for instance — rather than a standard nursing home visit where they would be more likely to experience the desolation of the elderly. But whenever or wherever students work with the elderly, it is crucial that they try to draw forth from older people the uniqueness they each have — their skills, their insight, their persons.

- Students can make a bulletin board display to build awareness that people still grow in old age. The display could feature famous people who accomplished significant things after the age of 69. Older students could do research projects on those older persons named above and others.

- Have students (middle-grade and older) read the following excerpt from the story of Ann Shadlow for an insight into a Native American perspective on older people. Answer the discussion questions that follow.

> I was raised by my grandparents. They had full control of us. We were raised real gentle. No harsh words. They would set us down and talk to us.
>
> My grandfather was French and Indian. His father was a French trader, and his mother a Cheyenne woman. My grandmother was English and Indian. She didn't speak English.
>
> We were taught and raised that older people came first. I think that my life is richer because I lived close to my grandparents. The aunts and cousins were all very good. I stayed around the old people and enjoyed them. My grandmother lived over the hill in her little log house. Grandmother's house had a dirt roof and floor. They destroyed the house when she died. My grandmother dressed me from the time I was little. We always dressed in our Indian clothes. I wore the long cotton skirts with dark prints and the little high

boots. She'd always tie bells on them so she'd know we were around.

> —Excerpted from the story of Ann Shadlow [Pretty Wing] from Oklahoma City, as recorded in *Growing Older,* by George Ancona, E. P. Dutton, 1978.

- What does she mean when she says "older people came first"?

- Is this different from the way most Americans think of older people?

- Do you think older people should come first?

5. *Visiting an older person:* Have students reflect on the following reading and decide whether and when they might be able to visit an older person. In a religious education situation, you might discuss the religious motivation for such an action.

A Reader's Hope: "I was in prison, you visited me." I am in prison — for the rest of my life. I can never escape. No one can free me. I have committed no crime.

My prison is not made of bars and walls. It is one of flesh, bones and blood…all mine. My body has become my prison. It never seemed like a prison when I was young. But something happened on the way to the forum! I became old. Why did I think it only applied to others?

The day finally comes when we look into a mirror with Snow White's familiar question. And the mirror answers honestly: we are no longer the fairest of them all. Is that really me? Why do I look so different from the way I feel?

Is there no solution to my dilemma? I told myself there were still things to do, places to go, and people to meet before I was ready to sleep. My flesh and blood prison sat in a chair, with a restless "me" inside, and life was passing me by.

How does one cope with sagging muscles, stiffened joints, aching parts which refuse to do our bidding even though the spirit is more than willing to go on? I never thought growing old would be like this.

The "me" who inhabits my prison has not changed that much. Inside, I wanted to take a brisk walk, go shopping, visit a friend, even do something daring, such as climb a mountain, swim an ocean, or soar to the moon.

Perhaps you are the answer. You can help me. Come to visit me. Let me smell your perfume.

Bring the crisp cold air of the outdoors inside to me. Play the music I want to hear. Read the news to me. Tell me about the world. Let's discuss a good book, a football game, the new look in fashion. I am hungry to know it all.

Above all, talk to me as an equal, rather than someone who has been reduced to basket-weaving or finger painting. My IQ has not turned white or even slightly gray. And please try not to look at me with pity in your eyes. My life has been gloriously full of adventures, joys, good times as well as bad.

When you must take your leave of me, refrain from patting my cheek like a small child. Give my hand a hearty shake instead. It may hurt my arthritic bones, but you will help me feel that I am still in the human race.

And come to see me next week. No appointment necessary.

— Madeleine Keen, 246 S. 1920 W., Provo, Utah; from *A.D.*, September 1980, United Church of Christ, 1840 Interchurch Center, 475 Riverside Drive, New York, NY 10115. Used with permission.

Further Resources

Annie and the Old One, by Miska Miles, illustrated by Peter Parnall, Little, Brown, 1971. Through her grandmother, a respected Navajo elder, Annie learns a valuable lesson about growth and change and death.

First Snow, by Helen Coutant, illustrated by Bo-Dinh, Knopf, 1974. This story of a small Vietnamese girl's relationship with her grandmother and the experience of her grandmother's death is full of gentleness and warmth.

Grandma's Wheelchair, by Lorraine Henriod, illustrated by Christa Chavalier, Albert Whitman, 1982. A delightful fun-filled book in which the Grandma is an active person, and her wheelchair is simply an aid.

My Grandson Lew, by Charlotte Zolotow, illustrated by William Pene Du Bois, Harper & Row, 1974. Lewis shares his happy memories of his grandfather with his mother. "He gave me eye-hugs...."

Wheels, by Jane Resh Thomas, illustrated by Emily Arnold McCully, Clarion Books, 1986. Five-year-old Elliot learns something about competition with the help of his grandfather.

Other Recommended Children's Books:

Younger Children:

Uncle Elephant, by Arnold Lobel, Harper & Row, 1981.

Grandma Is Somebody Special, written and illustrated by Susan Goldman, Albert Whitman, 1976.

Fish for Supper, written and illustrated by M.B. Goffstein, Dial Press, 1976.

Middle-Grade Children:

Grandpa — A Young Man Grown Old, by Harriet Langsam Sobol, photographs by Patricia Agre, Coward, McCann & Geohegan, 1980.

Grandmama's Joy, by Eloise Greenfield, illustrated by Carole Byard, Philomel Book, available from the Putnam Publishing Group, 1980.

Through Grandpapa's Eyes, by Patricia MacLachlan, illustrated by Deborah Ray, Harper & Row, 1979.

The Hundred Penny Box, by Sharon Bell Mathis, illustrated by Leo and Diane Dillon, Viking Press, 1975.

Growing Older, by George Ancona, E.P. Dutton, 1978.

Our Golda: The Story of Golda Meir, by David A. Adler, illustrated by Donna Ruff, Viking Press, 1984.

Older Children:

The Ways of Grandmothers, by Beverly Hungry Wolf, illustrated with photos, Morrow, 1980.

As We Are Now, by May Serton, W.W. Norton, 1973.

What About Grandma? by Hadley Irwin, Atheneum, 1982.

Adults:

Mother of the Year is a wonderfully inspiring film and video on the life of Ruth Youngdall Nelson, an 80-year-old grandmother who was voted U.S. "mother of the year" at age 70 and who was extremely active in peace and justice efforts until her death in 1984. Besides her personal witness of compassion and courage, Ruth shows how she was parented and how she parented her children in ways to nurture compassionate and courageous action.

While children will not understand all the issues she deals with, they will respond to her witness and vitality. Adults of all ages will be inspired, even if they have difficulty with the specific issues she addresses and the specific actions she took. Available as a rental from the Institute for Peace and Justice; to purchase or rent the film version, contact John de Graaf at KCTS-TV, 4045 Brooklyn Ave., N.E., Seattle, WA 98105.

One-hundred-year-old nursing home resident and kindergarten friend use pop-up cone puppets to enact "The Rabbit in the Moon" (see p. 61).

Nursing home resident and young friend use the frame to help "picture" a peaceful future brought about by things each decides to do now (see "Picture Me," p. 85).

Part IV

DISABILITY AWARENESS

25

The Perfeckt Kingdom

Theme and Format

This is a participatory puppet drama on the subject of individual strengths and weaknesses, talents and flaws, exemplary qualities and imperfections.

Cast

- GUARD
- DOG
- CAT
- VILLAGERS
- KING
- QUEEN
- NUMBER ONE, TEACHER
- NUMBER TWO, GIRL
- NUMBER THREE, OLD MAN
- NUMBER FOUR, BOY
- NUMBER FIVE, OLD LADY

THE PERFECKT KINGDOM

[SETTING: *The courtyard of the royal palace. The AUDIENCE may be invited to help manipulate the puppets and to add the cheers of the villagers and the sound effects for the dog and cat.*]

[*Enter* GUARD *followed by dog and cat.*]

GUARD: Make way! Make way for the king.

DOG: Bow wow! Woof woof!

CAT: Meow! Meow!

VILLAGERS: [*Wild cheers.*] Long live the king!

KING: Welcome. Welcome everyone. Today is the day of days.

QUEEN: What's today? Isn't it Monday?

KING: Of course it's Monday! It's the Monday of Mondays!

QUEEN: What does that mean?

KING: It means, of course, today is the Grand Contest. The splendid selection. The choosing of the chosen.

QUEEN: What? Monday?

KING: Have you forgotten? Today we choose the new court jester. The Royal Entertainer. The Star of Stars. The Position of Positions.

QUEEN: Oh, dear. Yes, of course, Monday.

KING: All are invited to bring forth their talents in a contest of abilities.

QUEEN: Oh, how exciting. I love contests!

VILLAGERS: [*Wild cheers.*] Hurrah! Long live the king.

DOG: Bow wow! Woof woof!

CAT: Meow! Meow!

KING: Everyone knows we live in the Perfect Kingdom and we enjoy the perfect life because, ahem, we have the perfect king!

QUEEN: Perfect? Well, er...ah...

KING: Perfect! That's what I said, P-E-R-F-E-C-T.

QUEEN: But dear, er, your Majesty...You...

KING: And as I was saying, I want only perfectly talented people. We are looking for the perfect court jester. Who is the first contestant?

GUARD: Number One, please. Number One.

[*Enter Number One,* TEACHER.]

DOG: Bow wow! Woof Woof!

CAT: Meow! Meow!

TEACHER: Here I am, your Majesty. I am Number One. I am a teacher.

KING: Good. Good. And what is your talent?

TEACHER: Well, in all modesty, I have many talents.

KING: Yes? Well, what can you do?

TEACHER: I can solve complex math problems. I can teach fractions, decimals, and algebra. I can calculate the distance to the stars.

KING: Wonderful. You have a great talent, a perfect talent. You will be a court jester and wizard combined! Are you sure you have no imperfections?

TEACHER: Quite sure... except for one or two minor things. One leg limps a little and I've always had a bit of asthma.

KING: A limp? Asthma? What's asthma?

TEACHER: It's a breathing problem, Your Majesty. Allergies to dust and molds that make it hard to breathe sometimes. But asthma has nothing to do with math. I'm a genius at math.

KING: So, you have a breathing problem, asthma, a limp... (sigh). And I did like the idea of a genius and wizard as the court jester... but I'm sorry. You don't qualify. You aren't perfect. Next.

GUARD: Number Two, please. Number Two.

[*Enter Number Two,* GIRL.]

DOG: Bow wow! Woof woof!

CAT: Meow! Meow!

[*The pretty girl steps forward and begins to dance a lovely dance. All the villagers applaud.*]

KING: Enchanting! Lovely, beautiful! You are perfect, my dear, perfect. You are surely the winner. A dancing court jester. Equality for women in this Perfect Kingdom. And such a pretty young girl.

GIRL: Th-th-th-th-thank you, Your Majesty. I-I-I knew you would l-l-like my dance. Of course, I s-s-s-stutter when I speak. A lot of people have s-s-s-speech problems. But s-s-s-speaking has nothing to do with d-d-d-dancing.

KING: A speech problem? Stutter? Oh dear, how unexpected. Such a beautiful dance, though. I am afraid you won't do, my dear. You see I am looking for the perfect person. Lovely talent, but you won't do. Next.

GUARD: Number Three, please. Number Three.

DOG: Bow wow! Woof woof!

CAT: Meow! Meow!

[*Enter Number Three,* OLD MAN, *carrying a painting under his arm.*]

OLD MAN: Here I am. A painter, Your Majesty. Look, this is my most recent painting. Quite good, don't you think?

KING: Yes, indeed. An artist. Exquisite! Perfect. Yes, yes... an excellent painting.

OLD MAN: Thank you, Your Majesty.

KING: An artist... how delightful! But wait. Are you wearing glasses?

OLD MAN: Certainly I am wearing glasses. They help me see the fine details.

KING: And, excuse me, but what is that in your ear?

OLD MAN: In my ear. Why, a hearing aid. After all, I am 82 years old.

KING [*shouting*]: You mean you can't hear me? Are you deaf?

OLD MAN [*startled*]: Of course I am able to hear you. That's what the hearing aid is for. It amplifies sound... all sound, including your shouting. It isn't necessary to shout into a hearing aid, you know.

KING: Oh, excuse me. I didn't know. I am sorry. But eyeglasses. A hearing aid. I guess you aren't perfect either. You don't qualify. Although your talent is very entertaining. Next.

GUARD: Number Four, please. Number Four.

DOG: Bow wow! Woof Woof!

CAT: Meow! Meow!

[*Enter Number Four,* BOY.]

BOY: That's me. About as perfect as you can get.

KING: You seem a little young for a potential court jester.

BOY: Well, I may be young, but I am the perfect athlete... the best in the kingdom. You name it. Football, baseball, soccer, basketball, tennis. I can swim and dive, too. Besides that... I'm handsome.

KING: Can you really do all those things? It sounds grand. I never was very good at sports. You certainly look perfect. Are you sure you are perfect?

BOY: Well, I'm the perfect athlete.

KING: That settles it. I'll choose you. I now award this royal certificate to you as the perfect court jester. Congratulations!

VILLAGERS: [*Wild cheers.*]

KING: Open it and read it.

BOY: [*Opens certificate and studies it closely.*] Um... it says...er...um...

KING: What? Don't you go to school? Can't you read?

BOY: [*Hesitates.*] I do go to school, Your Majesty. But the teacher says I have a reading problem. I can read if I take a long time and study the letters carefully. Sometime the way I see words is different from other people. In a special class I can read...but it's slow.

KING: Oh, no! And you looked so perfect! A reading problem! I guess you aren't perfect. Please return the scroll. You can't be the court jester. Next.

GUARD: The final contestant. Number Five, please. Number Five.

DOG: Bow wow! Woof woof!

CAT: Meow! Meow! Meow! Meow!

[*Enter Number Five,* OLD LADY.]

OLD LADY: Good afternoon, Your Majesty. I am Number Five.

KING: Someone nearer my own age. And what is your talent?

OLD LADY: I can sing. Would you like to hear a tune? [*Sings loudly.*]

KING: Lovely, wonderful. Fine singer. And after all, there aren't any other contestants. I will choose you. You seem perfect. Step forward.

OLD LADY: [*Steps forward, but trips.*] Woops. Excuse me. It's just my leg brace. I had polio when I was young. It's nothing...has nothing to do with my singing voice.

KING: A leg brace! Polio!

[*Suddenly the cat runs out in front of the king and queen and is followed by the dog. A wild chase occurs. All the contestants become involved in the chase. The villagers cheer. The dog chases the cat, the teacher chases the dog, the girl chases the teacher....All madly run around the king and the queen. The cat, in a desperate attempt to escape the dog, jumps up on the king's shoulder. Suddenly all the noise and movement halts. Silence. The cat's leap has dislodged the arm of the king as it is revealed to all that the king himself has a disability. An artificial arm!*]

KING: Oh, how humiliating! I'm so embarrassed! Now everyone can see...and everyone knows I'm not the perfect king. Long, long ago I lost my arm in battle. I'm so ashamed. Whoever heard of a king with only one arm?

QUEEN: That's all right, dear. You are a good king. And honest leaders are hard to find these days. You have many abilities and—like everyone else—some limitations. Losing an arm has nothing to do with being a good King.

AUDIENCE: Long live the king! [*Wild cheers.*]

KING: Thank you, thank you, everyone. Please bring all the contestants forward. Numbers One, Two, Three, Four, Five. I proclaim to all that you shall share your talents by taking turns as the court jester. On Monday the Teacher will entertain with mathematical games. On Tuesday the lovely girl will dance. On Wednesday the artist will paint. On Thursday the boy will perform athletic feats. On Friday the woman will sing her songs. And on the weekend the queen will recite poetry, her secret talent never revealed until today.

ALL PUPPETS: We all have handicaps and we all have abilities.

QUEEN: That's the way it is in the Perfeckt Kingdom...about the same as it is right here.

THE END

ƒ   ƒ   ƒ   ƒ   ƒ

ROYAL PROCLAMATION

You are an official member of the Perfeckt Kingdom.

You are hereby given the official title of

COURT JESTER

You have talents . . . and handicaps . . .

And so does everyone else.

ƒ   ƒ   ƒ   ƒ   ƒ

Discussion Questions

1. Why do you think the king only wanted a "perfect" person?

2. How did the contestants feel about their disabilities?

3. In what ways are you "less than perfect"?

4. How do you feel about these imperfections?

5. If you were the king, whom would you have chosen to be the court jester and why?

6. What do you think the Bible means when it says, "Blessed are you, Father, for revealing these things not to the learned and the clever but to the little ones" (Matthew 11:25)?

Follow-up Activities*

1. *Experimental simulations:* Teachers should ask for volunteers for each exercise and make it clear that a student may stop participating in a simulation at any time. Also explain that students will have an opportunity to experience to *some* extent what it is to be disabled, but that because they *can* stop, it is not really the same.

EXERCISE A: MOTOR DISABILITY

Post pictures showing a person in a wheelchair, another person using crutches, and a third person who has difficulty walking yet who does not use any aids. Ask students what problems they think someone who can get about only in a wheelchair might have in their school or community. The list might include inability to get into buildings, inability to reach materials on shelves, etc. Ask similar questions about people on crutches and about persons with motor problems who do not use aids. Write students' responses on the chalkboard.

Ask several student volunteers to spend the next school morning in wheelchairs, or on crutches with one leg fastened up with elastic. (Arrangements for borrowing equipment might be made with a hospital or service agency, or rental from a hospital supply store.) After the simulation, students should report to the class on their experiences. They should be asked what things they found difficult or impossible, how they felt when they couldn't perform a

---

*The following activities and reflection are excerpted from the *Bulletin* of the Council on Interracial Books for Children, vol. 8, nos. 6 and 7, 1977, and were written by Paula Wolff, a board member of the Disabled in Action and teacher of visually impaired pre-school children.

particular task, what help they needed — or didn't need — from their classmates. Classmates can also discuss their reactions to the volunteers.

Following the student presentations, invite one or more disability rights activists who have a motor disability to speak to the class about their experiences. Encourage students to check out their homes, apartment buildings, nearest movie house, etc., as to how accessible they are to disabled people.

EXERCISE B: SENSORY DISABILITY

Post pictures of persons who are blind, visually impaired, deaf, or hearing impaired. Ask students if they can tell the disability of the person in each picture. If students say they can't always tell or that the person isn't disabled, discuss how disabilities are not always visible or immediately apparent. Discuss particular problems people with "invisible disabilities" might have.

If you have not already done so, ask students what problems they think people with each of the disabilities mentioned might have in their school or community, and write down their responses on the chalkboard. The list might include inability to read signs, to hear announcements, to see the chalkboard, to read textbooks, to understand the teacher's instructions. Ask volunteers to spend the next morning blindfolded and to report to the class as in the previous exercise. The experience of a visually impaired — but not blind — person can be simulated by giving students photostats of a book page reduced to a small size plus hand magnifiers. Very young students can be given reduced pages showing shapes and asked to underline the triangles. Ask students how long it would take if they had to do all their reading this way, whether it made them tired, how they would feel having to take a rest using a magnifier and being expected to finish the text in the same time it took classmates who were not sight impaired. After the exercise, students can be shown a braille book and a large type book, raised line maps, etc. Discuss how such aids might be useful to persons with visual impairments.

Ask volunteers to wear earplugs (the kind used by swimmers) for part of the school day and then to report to the class on some of the problems they encountered.

Note: the degree of hearing impairment varies greatly among individuals. However, unlike totally blind persons, very few people are "stone deaf," that is, unable to hear anything at all. The more common disability is to hear with various degrees of difficulty.

2. *Uncovering stereotypes in TV programs, cartoons, comic cooks:* Give the class the assignment of looking at their favorite TV programs, cartoons, or comic books during the coming week to find out how they portray characters, people, or animals with disabilities.

Note: Many cartoons, comics, and TV programs "use" disabled characters for comic effect. Cartoons students can look for are Mr. Magoo (sight impairment), Porky the Pig (speech impairment), and Archie (developmental disability, learning disability). Have students share their feelings with the class at the end of the week. Ask students such questions as:

- How will watching programs that make fun of people who are mentally slower affect attitudes children have about people who don't learn things as quickly as others?

- How have you felt when someone made fun of you for not learning something fast enough?

3. *Presenting positive images:*

- Use the story of Helen Keller as a case study. One of the better biographies is *Helen Keller,* by Margaret Davidson, Scholastic, 1969, ages 7–11. Even this biography, however, omits coverage of Helen Keller's political activities.

- Students might also enjoy researching the story of a current actor with a disability. Linda Bove, who is deaf, is a good example. TABS: Aids for Ending Sexism in School, 744 Carroll St., #1D, Brooklyn, NY 11215, has a good article on her, as well as a poster. Younger children may know of her from her work on *Sesame Street.*

Further Resources

For Young Readers

The Balancing Girl, by Berenice Rabe, Dutton, 1981. Mobility impairment.

Darlene, by Eloise Greenfield, Methuen, 1980.

My Friend Jacob, by Lucille Clifton, Harper & Row, 1980. Mental retardation.

What's That? by Virginia Allen Jensen and Dorcas Woodbury Haller, Collins and World, 1980. Blindness.

Making Room for Uncle Joe, by Ada B. Litchfield, Whitman, 1984. Mental retardation.

For Middle Grades

Alesia, by Eloise Greenfield and Alesia Revis, Philomel, 1981. Mobility impairment.

Apple Is My sign, by Mary Riskind, Houghton Mifflin, 1981. Deafness.

Belonging, by Deborah Kent, Dial, 1978. Blindness.

Silent Dancer, by Bruce Hilbok, Messner, 1981. Deafness.

For Older Readers

Passing Through, by Corinne Gerson, Dial, 1978. Cerebral palsy.

Run, Don't Walk, by Harriet May Savitz, Watts, 1979. Mobility impairment.

Signs Unseen, Sounds Unheard, by Carolyn Brimley Norris, Alinda Press, 1981. Deafness.

The Swing, by Emily Hanlon, Bradbury, 1979. Deafness.

A Handful of Stars, by Barbara Girion, Laurel Leaf, 1981. Epilepsy.

APPENDIX:
MORE PUPPET IDEAS

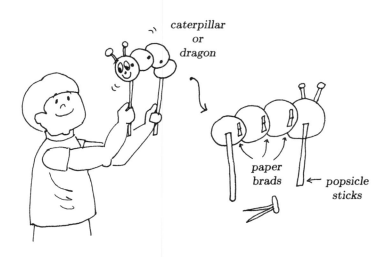

caterpillar
or
dragon

paper
brads

← popsicle
sticks

*"This little pig went
to market..."*

→ rubber or
garden glove

Body
Puppets
"Life-size"

Hand Puppet Pattern

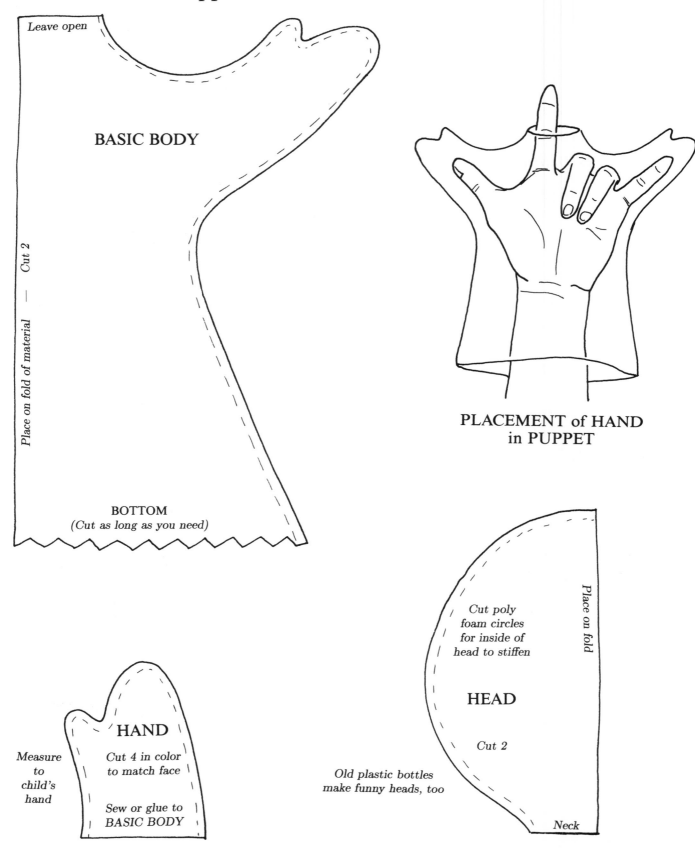

Leave open

BASIC BODY

Place on fold of material   —   Cut 2

BOTTOM
(Cut as long as you need)

**PLACEMENT of HAND
in PUPPET**

HAND

Measure
to
child's
hand

Cut 4 in color
to match face

Sew or glue to
BASIC BODY

*Cut poly
foam circles
for inside of
head to stiffen*

Place on fold

HEAD

Cut 2

*Old plastic bottles
make funny heads, too*

Neck

*Other Resources from
the Institute for Peace and Justice*

EDUCATING FOR PEACE AND JUSTICE, 1985 Edition

BY JAMES MCGINNIS, KATHLEEN MCGINNIS, AND OTHER CONTRIBUTORS

Volume 1: National Dimensions

12 Units ($14.25, 304 pages)

- Nonviolent Conflict Resolution
- Case Studies in Nonviolence
- Institutional Violence
- Peace and Justice in Schools
- Peace and Justice and the Law
- Poverty in the U.S.
- Sexism
- Racism
- Disabled People
- Older People
- Advertising/Stewardship
- Multicultural Education

Volume 2: Global Dimensions

8 Units ($14.25, 320 pages)

- World Hunger
- Global Poverty and Development
  (Case Study on El Salvador)
- Global Interdependence
- U.S. Foreign Policy
  (Case Studies on the Philippines and Nicaragua)
- Sadako and the Thousand Paper Cranes
  (Readers' Theater Version)
- U.S. – U.S.S.R. Relations
- The Military and U.S. Life
- War and Alternatives.

Volume 3: Religious Dimensions

6 Units ($14.25, 240 pages)

- Today's Peacemakers
- Peace and Justice
- The Prophets
- Gospel Culture Contrasts
- Peace and War
- Service Programs

All volumes contain:

- explanation of EPJ methodology
- a list of helpful organizations

Each unit of all 3 volumes contains:

- development of the basic concepts of the theme
- teaching strategies for all age levels
- a wide variety of action possibilities,
  both within the school and in the larger community
- short student readings and worksheets
- bibliography of further teacher and student resources
- directions on teaching the unit

All 3 volumes: $37.00 (price includes postage)

BUILDING SHALOM FAMILIES:
CHRISTIAN PARENTING FOR PEACE AND JUSTICE

A comprehensive parenting program that assists participants in dealing with important issues confronting today's families. By using creative visuals, music, stimulating presentations, prayerful reflections, and practical "how to" sessions, the video enables the participants to experience the McGinnises and their important message of how to build peace in the home. There are visual backgrounds for the McGinnises' input, which include documentary footage and still shots. Also included are short reflective pieces incorporated into the sessions that provide a fuller sensory experience of the themes.

BUILDING SHALOM FAMILIES (1986) is a complete video package containing the following materials for program leaders:

- two 120-minute 1/2" VHS videotapes
- a 32-page guidebook
- the *Parenting for Peace and Justice* book
- worksheets and action brochures
    - ☐ The Building Shalom Families Program — complete kit: $149.95 (plus $5 U.S. mailing)
    - ☐ "Peacemaking in the Home" Tape — 72 minutes with introductions and seven segments: $30.00
    - ☐ Additional sets of the guidebook, worksheets, action brochures, catalogues: $8.00

FAMILY ENRICHMENT MATERIALS

- **PARENTING FOR PEACE AND JUSTICE** is Kathy and Jim McGinnis's account of their own family experience and that of twelve other families in making justice and peace an integral part of family life. Chapters are Stewardship/Simplicity, Nonviolence in the Family, Helping Children Deal with Violence, Multiculturalizing Family Life, Sex-Role Stereotyping, Family Social Action, Prayer and Parenting, and How the Church Can Encourage Families. ($10.50)

- **STARTING OUT RIGHT: NURTURING YOUNG CHILDREN AS PEACEMAKERS,** by Kathy McGinnis and Barbara Oehlberg (Meyer-Stone Books, 1988) adapts the original PPJ book to families with pre-school age children. ($12.20)

- **CHILDREN AND NONVIOLENCE,** by Janet and Robert Aldridge (Hope Press, 1987), recounts the Aldriches experience raising ten children to be peacemakers. ($10.50)

- **CONFLICT PARTNERSHIP,** by Dudley Weeks (Transworld Productions, 1984), offers adults very practical techniques for nonviolent conflict resolution applicable to family, work, and community conflict situations. ($10.50)

- **FAMILIES IN SEARCH OF SHALOM** is a 100-frame 10-minute filmstrip introducing the PPJ themes and their Judaeo-Christian foundation. It has three new versions, adapting the script to Jewish, Black, and Hispanic audiences. ($29.00)

- **EXPANDED PHIL DONAHUE SHOW VIDEOTAPE** includes a 3-minute segment on family meetings as well as segments on how family support groups operate, on the PPJ Network, the *Families in Search of Shalom* filmstrip, and the 45-minute highly entertaining Donahue Show on PPJ. ($45.00)

PPJ NETWORK

The PPJN is a network of families, family life leaders, and others working with families with three main goals: to help families (1) understand how forces like violence, racism, materialism, and sexism affect them; (2) find ways of resisting these forces; and (3) do this as a whole family and with other families.

The PPJN is currently working through local PPJ coordinators and ecumenical local teams in some 150 U.S. and Canadian cities, plus 16 national Christian denominations. Families and leaders from other religious and moral traditions are also part of the PPJN. The PPJN offers a variety of services, from leadership training workshops and family enrichment experiences to linking families in the same area in "family support groups."

PPJN NEWSLETTER

The Newsletter, a 6-times-a-year resource, provides practical suggestions for family action, "parent-to-parent" reflection on efforts to live PPJ values, information on written and AV resources for both adults and children, suggestions for integrating family social action and prayer, and details about up-coming events (PPJ workshops, family camps, training events, etc.) Each issue of the newsletter focuses on a particular theme (e.g., nonviolence in the home, toys, families and the nuclear threat, families confronting racism). There are columns written by single parents and grandparents ("Grandparenting for Peace and Justice"!), and others. Members of the PPJN are strongly encouraged to share through the newsletter their own stories about applying PPJ to their family situation.

For a listing of all PPJ resources and information on how to become part of the PPJN and receive the PPJN newsletter and other mailings, send a self-addressed stamped envelope to:

Parenting for Peace & Justice Network
Institute for Peace & Justice
4144 Lindell Blvd., Room 122
St. Louis, Missouri 63108
Tel.: 314-533-4445